The Roaming Studio's Step-by-Step Guide to Drawing Faces

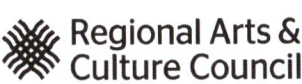 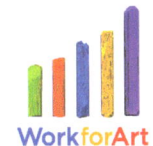

Copyright © 2015 Leah Kohlenberg

All rights reserved. No part of this publication may be reproduced, distributed, or transmitted in any form or by any means, including photocopying, recording, or other electronic or mechanical methods, without the prior written permission of the publisher, except in the case of brief quotations embodied in critical reviews and certain other noncommercial uses permitted by copyright law.

For permission requests, write to the publisher, addressed "Attention: Permissions Coordinator" at the address below.

Kiko Productions Ltd
P. O. Box 1806 - 00502 Nairobi, Kenya
www.kikopro.com

Ordering Information:

Quantity sales: Special discounts are available on quantity purchases by schools, libraries, corporations, associations, and others.

For details, contact the publisher at the address above.

Printed in the UK

This book was published with a professional development grant awarded by the Regional Arts and Culture Council in Portland, Oregon, in 2015. More details on their many grant programs and activities are here: http://www.racc.org/

Credits:

Design & Layout: Kennedy Kamau

Photography: Stephanie Wiarda

Stephanie Wiarda is a Portland, Oregon resident devoted to the arts for many years as gallery owner, arts administrator, silversmith, and photographer. You can find out more about her work at www.swiarda.com

ISBN 978-9966-1874-0-6

Dedication

This book is dedicated to all my students, past, present and future, who continue to learn with me with patience, grit and determination, as we tackle this art thing together. I'd also like to thank my amazing models for posing for the exercises of this book, Marc Kochanski, Malee Kenworthy and Rahul Rastogi. And I am ever so grateful to the midwife, you know who you are ...

This book is for teens and adults who have decided to pick up where they left off- most likely in grade school, or even before. They are professional people who've had success in their careers, and drawing is the new challenge for them. They fear it a little, but they also feel ready to conquer it and/or they've decided art needs to be included in their lives. And they are looking for practical help in learning how to develop their art skills. They may or may not have significant experience drawing faces - what they share is a desire to get better at the skill, regardless of their experience level. They are willing to put in at least three hours weekly to improving their drawing, if not more!

INDEX

2	Introduction
4	Setting up Your studio
5	Materials List
6	Before you begin: taking a good selfie
8	Construction and Basic Face Measurements
12	Shading / Face Planes Features
14	Features
23	Step by Step 1: Drawing the Face in Pencil
37	Step by Step 2: Drawing the Face in Charcoal
45	Step by Step 3: Drawing the face in pen and ink

INTRO

This book is not a creative book. You've already got that, it's what caused you to pick up this book in the first place. This book is a technical book. It's designed to take the mystery out of portraiture, and give you some helpful tips on how to improve the likeness of the faces you draw. This is a good book for artists of all levels, especially beginners and those who taught themselves to draw from a young age.

We like to think that drawing is a so-called "talent" that is inherited, like blue eyes, or a dislike of broccoli. Nothing could be further from the truth.

Drawing is a skill that is cultivated purely by practice, and learning the rules by which it operates. Rules? You might ask yourself. **Drawing has rules?** Indeed, drawing is ruled by our visual and spatial perception, commonly known as our right brain. (Though we now know that the brain is so flexible these functions can operate on any side of the brain). Learning how to see the shapes and values of a thing correctly is the drawer's biggest challenge.

Proportion and measurement are our primary tools to help us draw more accurately. Perhaps surprisingly to you, all human faces have basically the same measurements. That's right - our eyes sit in roughly the same place, as do the rest of our features. Characteristics that seem quite distinctive when focused on closely - like close-set eyes, an upturned nose, or ears that stick out - are in actuality different by only a millimeter or two.

So knowing the measurements can help you draw the face, because if we know where things are, and mark them lightly on the paper, then our faces will have a better likeness when they are finished. This is what we call construction. It's a different way of drawing than that of the self-taught drawer, who learns how to draw by moving from tiny detail to tiny detail - first drawing the eye, then the other eye, then the nose, and so on and so on. That way of working will only get you so far. Once you are unable to interpret what you see correctly, the self-taught drawer has no way to handle complex a three-quarter pose, for example, which involves foreshortening, proportions and perspective.

With construction, on the other hand, we start with the larger simple shapes, and then use that as a template to help locate the smaller shapes within. Only then do we start working on details. It's like building a table. You wouldn't just try to guess how long each leg is as you are cutting it, right? You use a ruler to determine accurate measurements. It works the same way with the face. When you know where things are, it becomes easier to draw.

The exercises of this book follow The Roaming Studio art method: doing the subject (the face) in three different mediums. Each medium highlights different principles in drawing. You won't be good at all the mediums equally, but you will learn something new from each of them.

Don't expect your drawings to exactly mirror the samples in the book, or if you do this with a friend, don't expect your two drawings to look alike. That's Ok. In fact, that is your creative voice pushing through. As long as you use the techniques I teach you in the book correctly, you should get likeness. Beyond that, your work should still show your own marks, **your own way of making lines, its own sense of character.**

That's why this book isn't a creative book. You don't need a book to access your creativity and your voice, which is just in you, and always present. What you need to learn is the technique. Drawing isn't a magical ability that only a rare few have to know what and where to put things down on paper. It involves measuring, math, understanding and evaluating proportions, correctly identifying shapes, and mark making. It also involves making a lot of mistakes - just as it is when we learn to read, write or do math, or even learn to talk - before we get it right. For this reason, it's a fantastic skill for just about anyone to get better at, if they practise diligently. **This skill isn't just good for artists. It's good for writers, police officers, teachers, psychologists - anyone who wants to improve their ability to perceive people and situations clearly.**

The most profound gift I hope you take from this book, besides the fact that virtually anyone can learn to improve their drawing, is that although we notice a tremendous variety in the faces of the world, faces are basically the same, and the differences that we notice are small, tiny shifts. I was teaching drawing to a teenage boy recently who had been in a car accident when young. Skin from his forehead was taken to heal injuries in his eye.

His drawing showed a dramatically tilted right eye, running down the side of his face, parallel to his nose.

"Wait a second," I told him. "Your eye doesn't look like that."

He pointed to a picture with an ever so slight tilt, and said, "Look it's there."
So I took the pencil from his hand and corrected it, to the millimeter shift it was off from center. "See?" I said. "That's what your eye looks like. Virtually the same as your left eye."
And he looked at me with surprise.

That, my friends, is the major magic you'll find in drawing. To realize that your perception of what makes you different is just a perception, and not the reality. We should all learn how to see so well.

SETTING UP THE STUDIO

You have several options for setting up your studio when working on the exercises in this book. You can work flat on the table - necessary when using ink, and manageable when working with the small paper sizes.

However, a flat table can skew your perspective (because the further the paper is from you the smaller and more angled away it seems.) An easel - either table top or standing - and large boards will keep both your source material and your drawing straight up and down, relieving the skewing and allowing you to see and draw more accurately. See photos below:

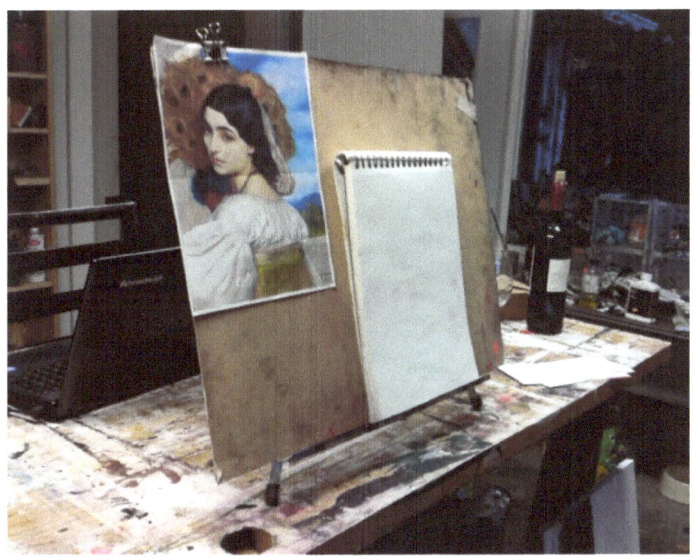
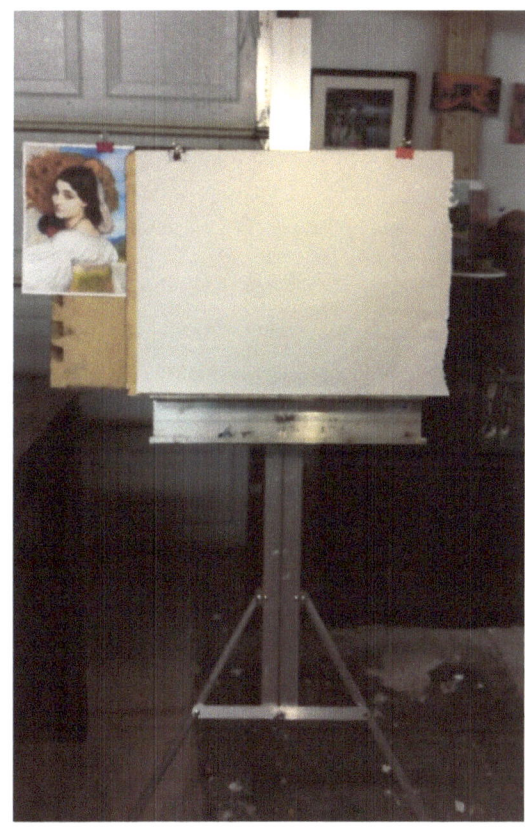

MATERIAL LIST

For the exercises in this book, you'll need the following materials:

hb, b, 2h, 2b and 4b lead pencils

Erasers
kneaded, gum, rubber and vinyl

A bamboo pen and bamboo brush

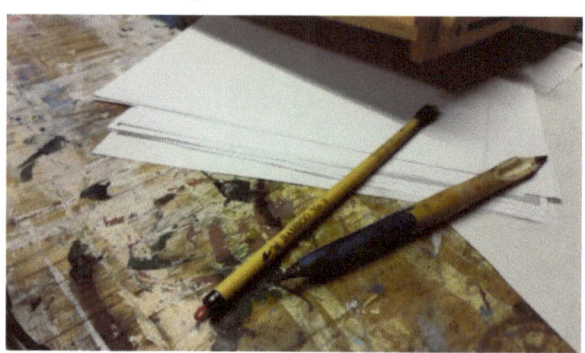

Non waterproof black drawing ink
(I like Higgins)

Charcoal
both vine, and willow, including thick and thin sizes, soft, medium and hard

Paper
drawing, newsprint, Bristol
(both 9X 12 inches or 22X30 cms, and 18 X 24 inches or 45X60 cms):

Size Does Matter!
For most people, the immediate comfort zone of drawing is to use paper roughly the same size as the photo source you are working from. While I would recommend that the first time through with these exercises, I'd then suggest going through again with a larger size paper, forcing you to scale up. What you'll learn through this exercise is that the measurements I'm teaching you are what allow you to make a drawing any size. As long as everything is proportional, a halfway point is still a halfway point!

BEFORE YOU BEGIN ....

Taking a good selfie ...

Sometimes, the easiest subject to practice on is yourself, and the easiest way to snap a photo is with a selfie. But it's easy to get angles wrong with a selfie, resulting in skewed proportions.

Some tips, for getting the best face-forward shot: Note the ears are of about equal size on either side of the face. Eyes can be looking anywhere. Arm should be straight out, not at an up or down angle

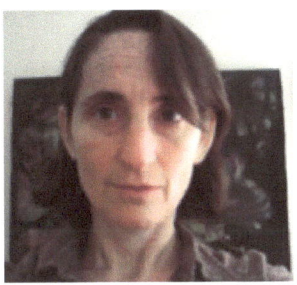

Some things NOT to do with your photo:

This photo has chopped the top of the head off, which will mess up your measurements; the photo on the right appears to be face forward, but in fact is slightly tilted (you can see this by noticing that the ears are not of equal size, or don't appear to be of equal size?)).

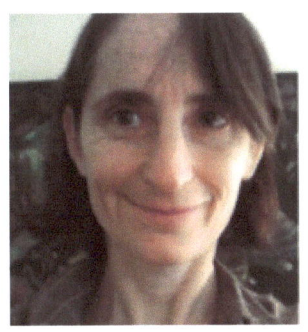 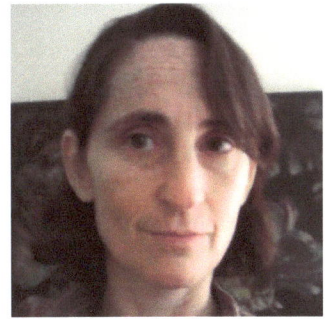

This photo, taken by the same person with a different camera, has elongated the features (compare with the top photo) which messes with the measurements you'll learn about in Chapter 1. Sometimes this happens because of the angle you hold the camera. If the features seem off in the photo, check your face in the mirror, holding a pencil out with a straight arm to check measurements

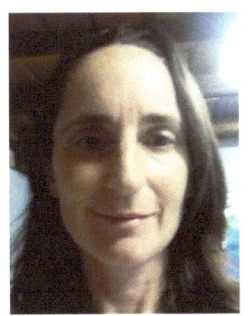 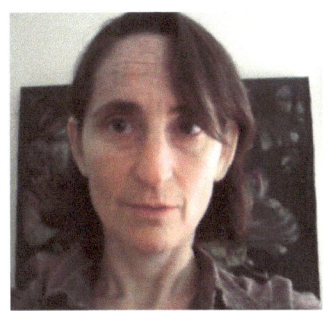

Construction and Basic Face Measurements

CONSTRUCTION

Believe it or not, the adult human face has a fairly universal construction, meaning generally features are in about the same place in all faces*?) When I teach drawing classes, particularly to beginners or self-taught artists, it's not uncommon for the students to shoot me a look of complete betrayal when they realize this: **I didn't know we were going to do math,** I've heard more than once.

But this is the smart way to draw, and it's a method the best professional artists employ. **Knowing the larger general shapes of things,** and identifying where the features sit on the face, is the first step to drawing the face. It may be tough to incorporate at the beginning, but as you practice these ideas, they will become second nature to you.

We are going to focus on drawing the face in a forward position, because it's simpler and the construction is less complex. But I did want to review for you what I mean by large simple shapes and the basic construction of the face in all positions. Your first lines when drawing should be the overall shape of the face, but not the details. Instead, **draw a simple shape that serves as the envelope** within which the entire face fits.

When you look at a face from straight in front, **the shape is an egg-shape, a little bit wider on top, and slightly narrower on the bottom** (avoid a pointy bottom and dramatic curves, remember, **changes to the face register as giant changes to the eye**):

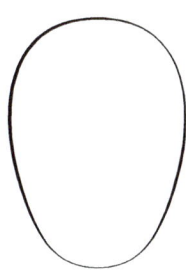 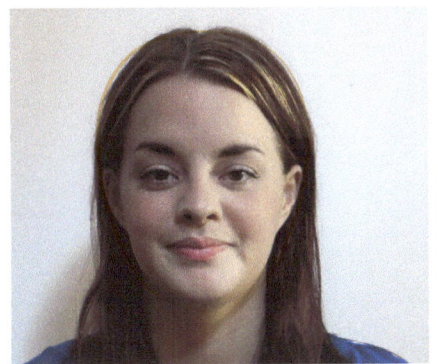 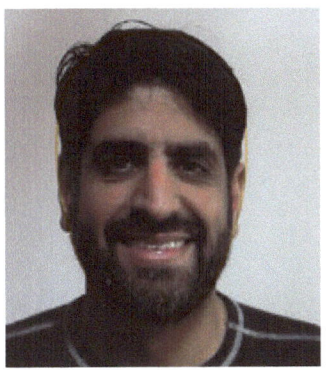

Note that this egg shape goes over the OUTSIDE of the ears.

For the three-quarter pose, where the face is turned away, the shape is a circle on its side, and series of curved and straight lines, like this:

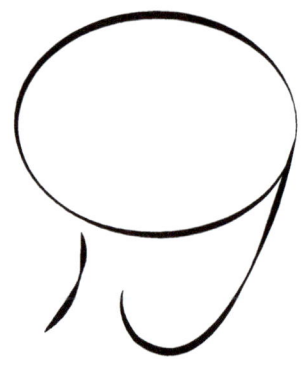 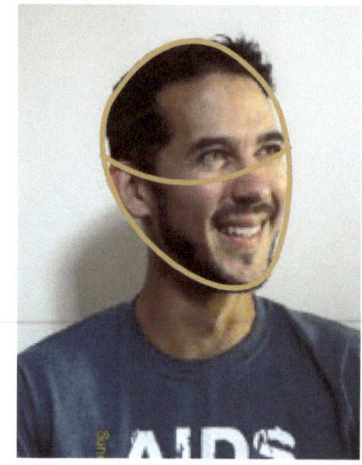 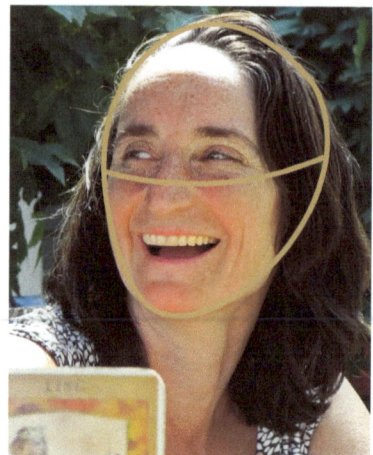

So our first step in drawing involves sketching in these big construction envelopes, within which we will carve out the shape of the face. I encourage you, if you are working from a photograph, to sketch these shapes on the photo first, because it's easier to see them, and then redraw them on your blank paper.

For those of you working with big paper, remember, as you are sizing up, **the proportion of one shape to the other should be the same.**

The roaming studio's step-by-step guide to drawing faces

MEASUREMENTS OF THE FACE

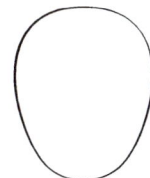

Draw an egg shape for the head.

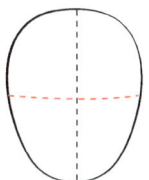

Find the halfway point, this is the middle of the eye-line

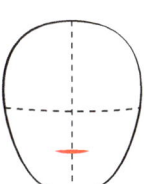

Halfway point between the eyeline and the bottom of the face/chin. This marks the bottom of the nose, or just below it

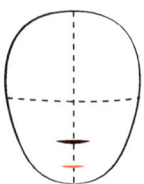

Halfway point between the bottom of the nose and the bottom of the face/chin. This is generally the bottom of the lips.

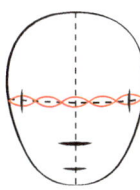

The eye line is 5 equal eyes across, from the tip of one ear to the tip of the other ear. First, draw a line bisecting the halfway point of each corner eye.
NOTE: to make sure this line is the appropriate length, employ Step 4 a and b on page 24. Then divide that line into five equal lengths. There is one eye length between each eye, and then one eye length on either side of the eye, going all the way to the tip of the ear

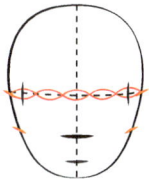

The ears start at the top of the eyeline, at halfway point of the corner eye. they end lined up with or just above the bottom of the nose, add lines just above the bottom of the nose. add lines marking the top and bottom of the ear as shown

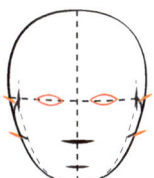

Here is where things start to vary. You'll shape the ears and carve the jawline from within the bottom of the circle, as shown with the dotted lines (note, everyone's jawline has a different shape).

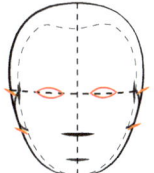

Add the hairline, as shown by the dotted lines.
(Once again, remember that everyone's hairline is shaped differently and located differently). If a person has long or big hair, that will fall outside of the circle, so sketch in the outer shapes of the full hairline where they fall in relation to the original face-shape circle you drew.

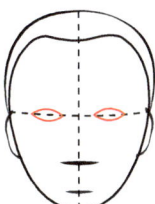

The roaming studio's step-by-step guide to drawing faces

Faces seem so different yet we are all so close to the same when it comes to features placement: lets see how the measurements layout on these four faces:

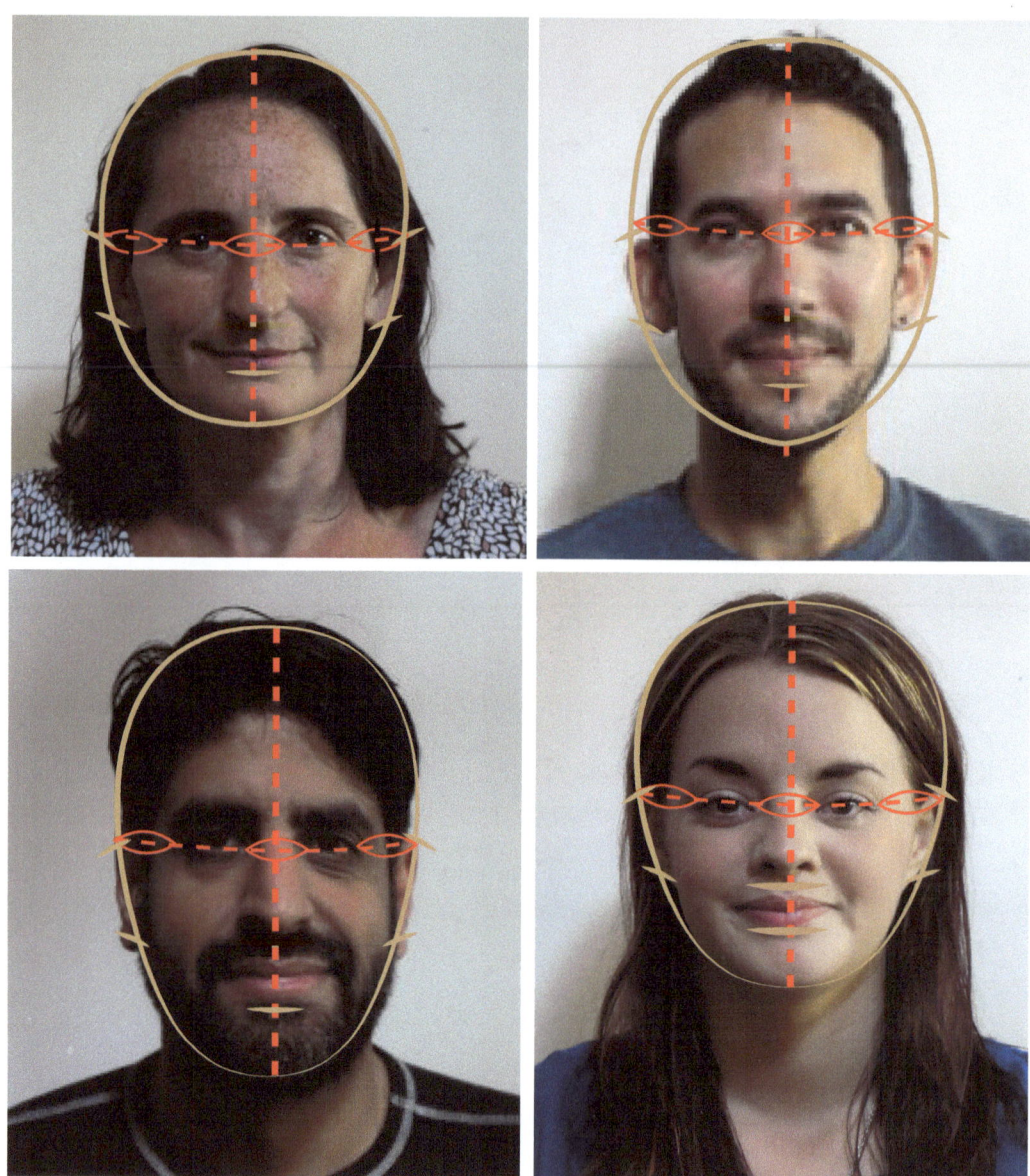

SHADING AND FACE PLANES

One of the hardest things to see in the face is the heavy amount of shading happening there. We see the face as one big, flat object, but in fact, only small parts of the face are actually unshaded - these are the areas that stick out towards the light, such as the middle ridge of the nose, the bottom lip, the top of the head where the skull meets the hairline, for example. The rest of the face must be shaded, particularly everything under the eye sockets. And since the skin is stretched tight over the muscles and bones of the skull, shading is a subtle and complex task.

A basic shading map looks like this

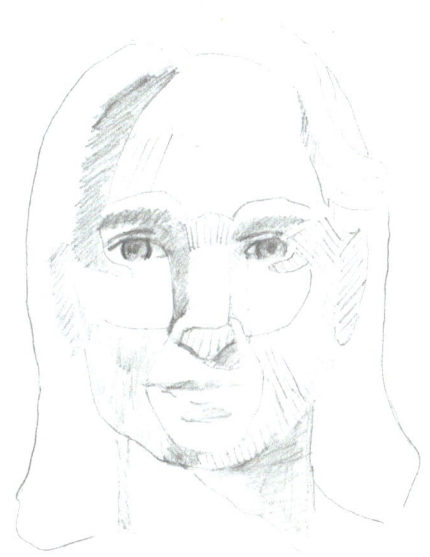

Graphic A (shading / Planes Map)

To understand face shading, you need to understand face planes. What is a plane? Quite simply, a plane is an area that points in the same direction towards the light. Once the area changes direction, a new plane is created. And that new plane, because it is facing in a different direction from the light, is lit and shaded differently than the plane next to it.

Planes are easy to see in a cube:

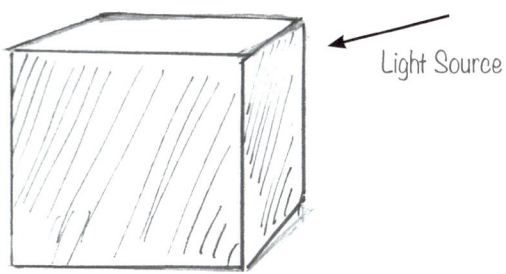

Graphic B (shading / planes)

And it's even easier to see how the light might change on each plane, depending on what direction the light is facing.

Planes are a little tougher to determine in a sphere:

Because there is no sharp edge determining where the side of the sphere ends, we mark the plane change where the sphere starts to turn away from the light, and we note it for the light changes there.

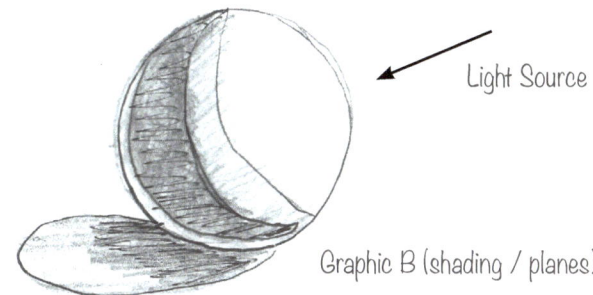

Graphic B (shading / planes)

There are very few lines on the face, but there are a lot of shading shifts that follow the bumps and hollows of the cranium. But to see them it takes training.

That's why the face planes models have been developed. Admittedly, they look a little robotic and strange (And you'll understand why we have virtually no hard lines on the face, when you see them). But these exaggerated planes show us where to look for the subtle twists and turns of the face itself. Once you've worked with this model, you'll see them more clearly in the real face.

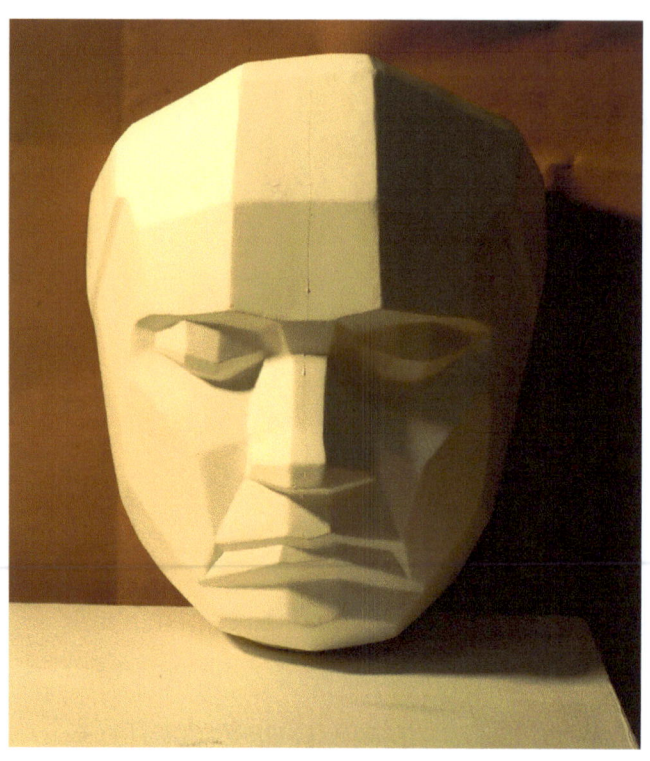
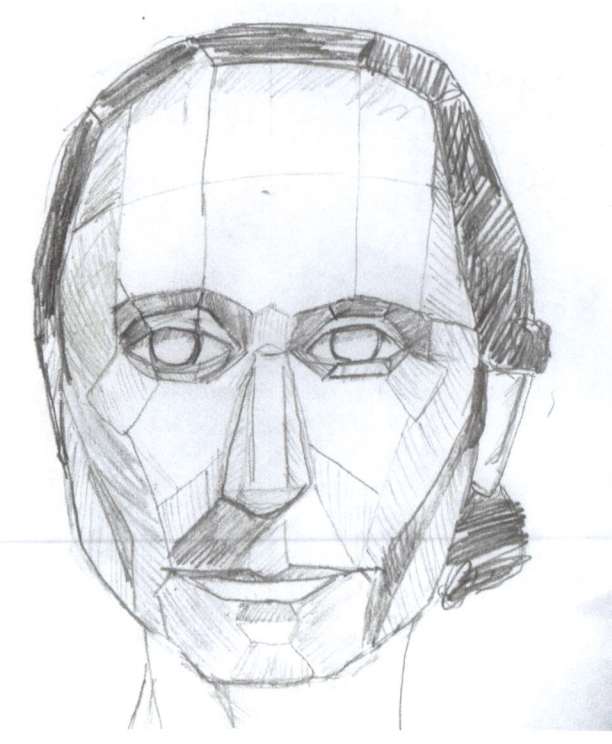

Exercise 1:

Using the three face plane samples, print out your own face, and draw in the planes on top of it (as in the face below)

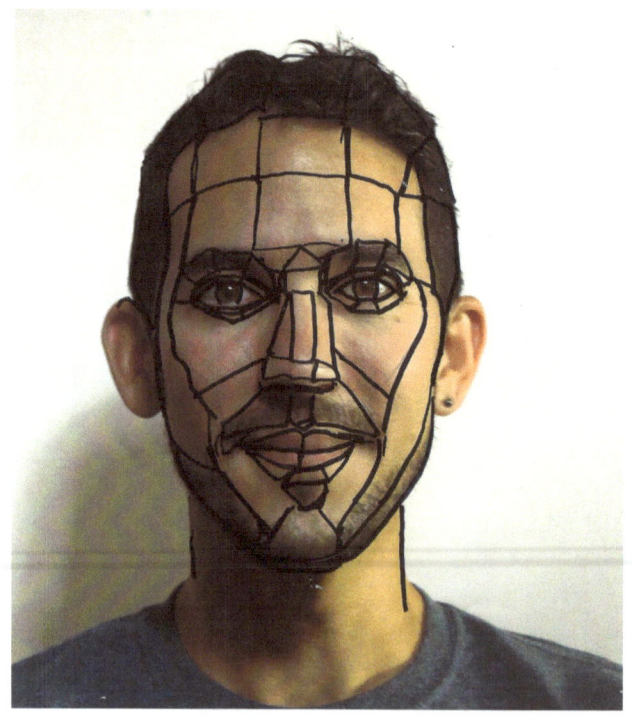

The roaming studio's step-by-step guide to drawing faces

FEATURES

One of the surprising things about the face is how the features are so similarly placed. What makes for the dramatic differences between us? Small tweaks to the features can add to some very noticeable changes. We can review these, as well as tips on drawing the features, below:

EYES:

Remember how we drew eyes when we were kids? Two curved lines in an almond shape, a perfectly round iris, and many projecting, single eyelash lines? (see graphic A below)

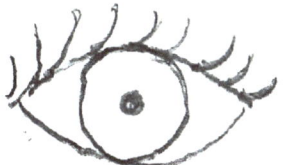

Graphic A

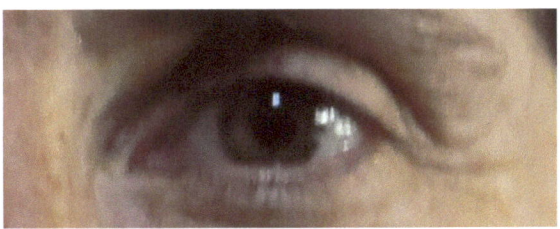

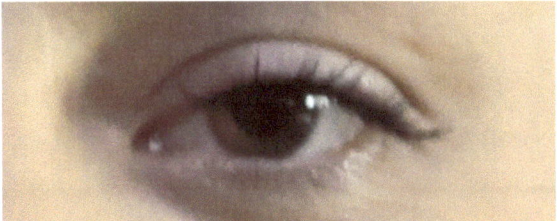

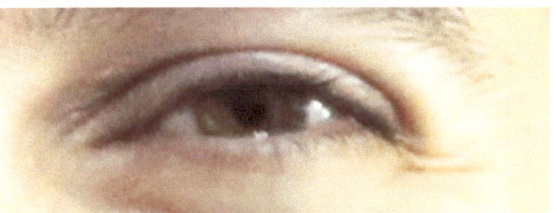

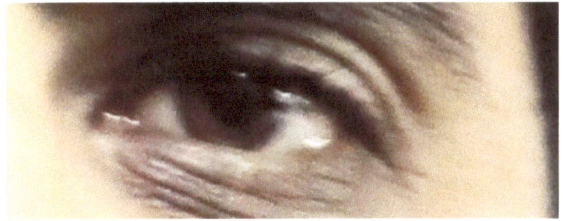

In fact, it's only the top eye line that's curved, while the bottom line is mostly straight - and not quite as visible (because the lower lid pokes out and catches the light). As well, unless we are holding our eyes wide open in a look of surprise, the top and bottom of the iris are covered by the lids, so we see only two curved lines
(see graphic B below).

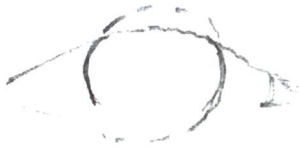

Graphic B

A distinctive difference is the crease above the upper lid - for some, there is skin between the upper lid and the crease, for others, the crease runs right into the upper lid

(see graphic C above).

The iris has a dark line around the edge, regardless of eye color. It's nearly as dark as the pupil.

The upper lid shades both the upper white and iris areas of the eye, so lightly shade the white areas and the iris - the bottom half of the iris is a touch lighter. There is also always a white highlight on or around the pupil - just leave this area white if you can. The upper eyelashes are usually portrayed as a thicker, soft dark line, getting narrower as you move towards the tear duct. The lower lashes are usually portrayed just below the light lower lid line, and from the edge of the eye to about the center of the iris. When drawing the eye, avoid using hard lines whenever possible, even when you see them distinctly. The best drawings soften all the lines of the face.

FEATURES STEP-BY-STEP (EYES)

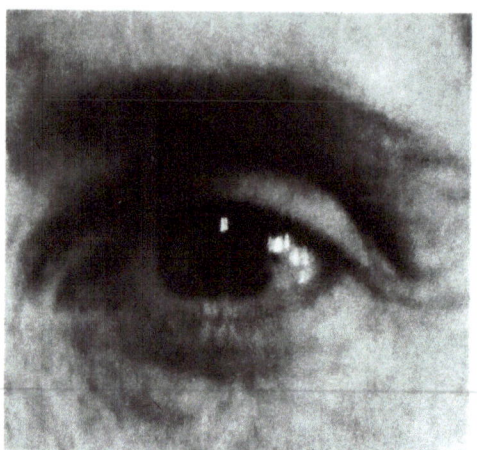

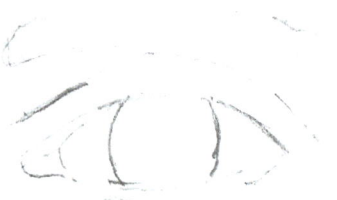

Step 1: Draw the outline of the eye, and the upper lid and the iris

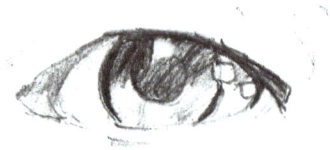

Step 2: Darken the iris and the pupil, add a white reflected light in one upper corner of the eye. Shade the top of the iris and the white darker. Make the iris lighter directly diagonally and down from the white reflected light

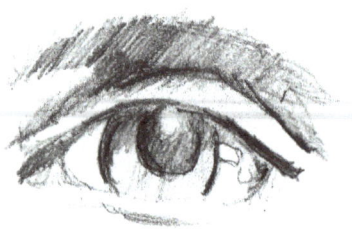

Step 3: Add a thick line on the top lid to delineate eyelashes. Shade the tear duct. Soften the upper lid line. Lighten the bottom lid with your eraser.

The roaming studio's step-by-step guide to drawing faces

NOSE:

My friend Lado Pochkhua, an artist from the Republic of Georgia, once told me a seminal truth about noses. "Leah," he said. "There are two types of noses: foxes and pigs." Which one are you? (see graphic A below).

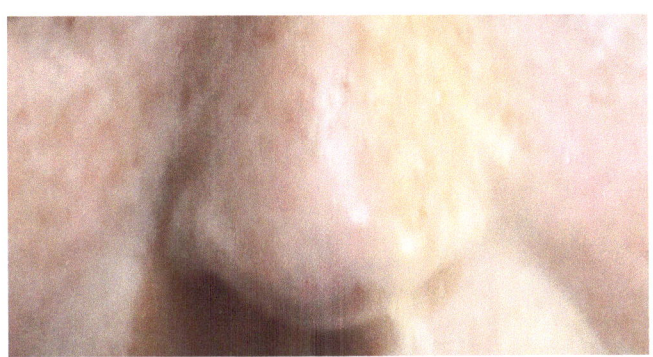
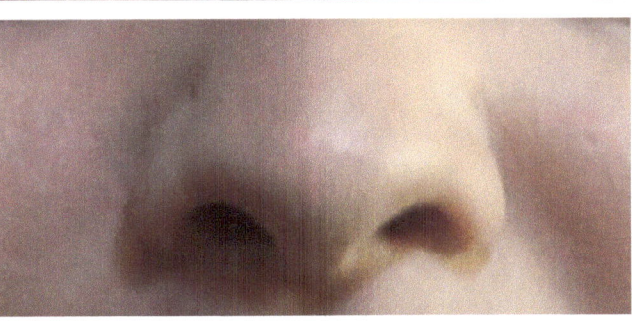
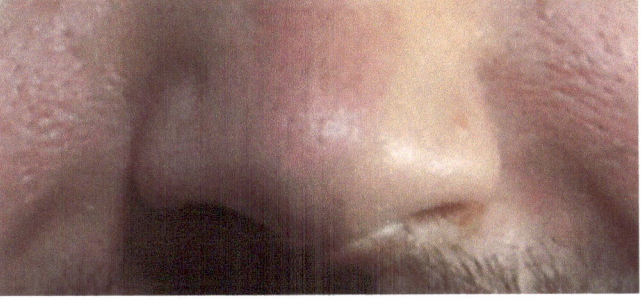
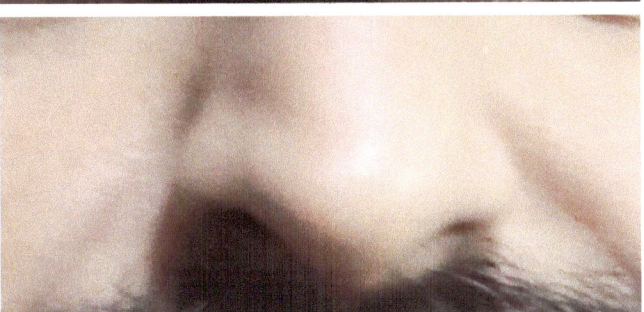

This means the outer nostril lines are either above the bottom of the nose (fox), or straight across, showing more nostril (pig). Much of the nose is created via soft shading; along the sides of the nose, the bottom of the nose, and the shadow underneath, depending on which direction the light is facing. Start by lightly shaping the outer nostril lines and bottom shape of the nose.

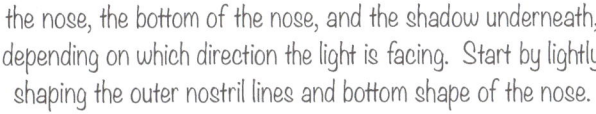

(Graphic B below)
Then shade in the entire bottom tip of the nose, VERY lightly darkening the nostrils (de-emphasize the dark areas of the nostrils, drawing them smaller than they appear). Pull out the reflected light in the inside of the nostrils. (Graphic C- below)

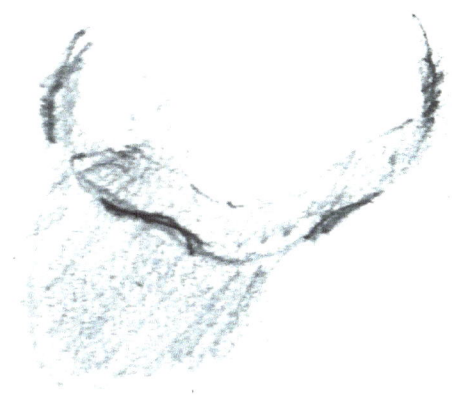

Graphic C

The roaming studio's step-by-step guide to drawing faces

Features Step-by-Step (Nose)

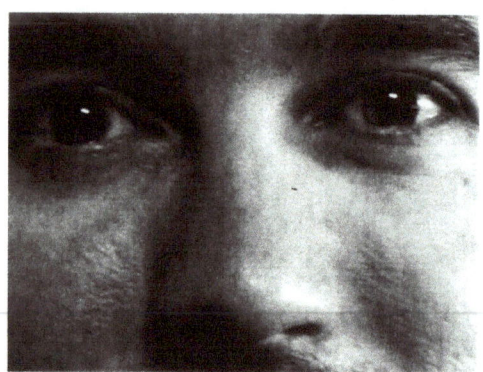

Step 1: Line up the side nostril lines with the tear duct of each eye. Note the shape: are they a fox, or a pig?

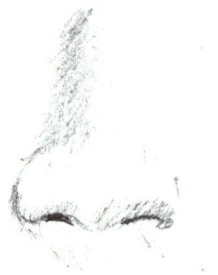

Step 2: Drawing the bottom outer shape of the nose, from side nostril to side nostril. Lightly shade in the cast shadow under the nose. Shade the sides of the nose, the bottom tip of the nose, and VERY lightly delineate the nostril lines with a small dark line. Make these dark areas smaller and less distinct than they appear in reality.

MOUTH:

Mouths are another area of difference. Some people have thin lips, others thick. Pay attention to these shapes when you draw them. (See graphic A - Mouths below)

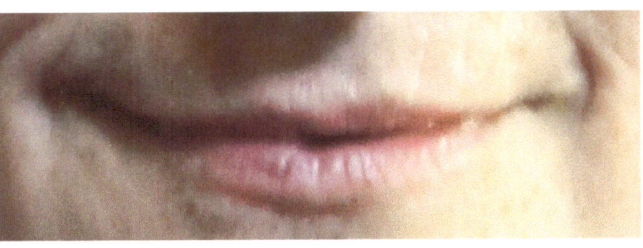

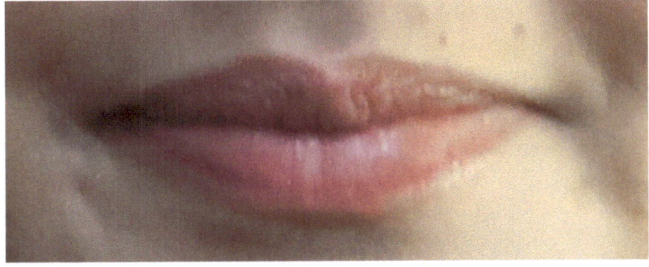

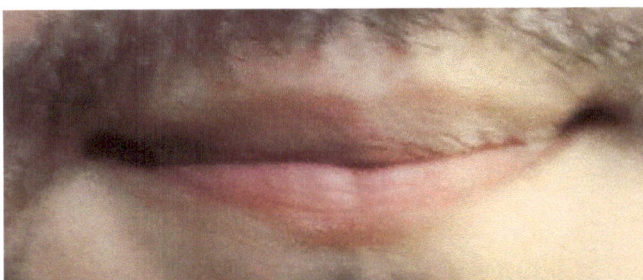

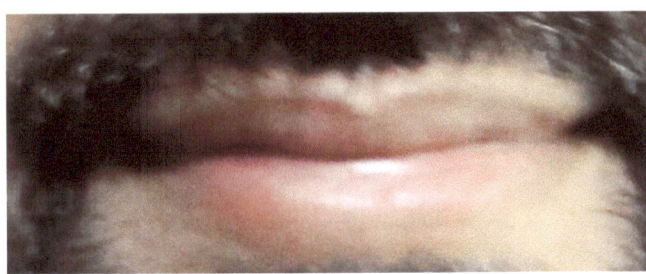

In general, the middle line of the mouth (between the upper and lower lip) is darker, but still draw it softly and as a broken, slightly curvy line. (see graphic B - mouths below).

Note that this soft middle line extends beyond the end of the upper and lower lip, into a little dark crease that lines up with the middle of the iris. In general, the upper lip is darker (because it is

Graphic B

turning away from the light), and the lower lip is medium shaded towards the top, and very light towards the bottom (because it is turning towards the light). Usually, don't delineate strongly the bottom lower lip line, particularly on the lighter side of the face. There is also a little light area that follows the curve of the upper lip. (See graphic C - mouths below).

If the person is smiling open-mouthed, teeth are another thing - like nostril holes, that we de-emphasize. The only thing to focus on is a slight graying in the upper teeth area, and maybe shading

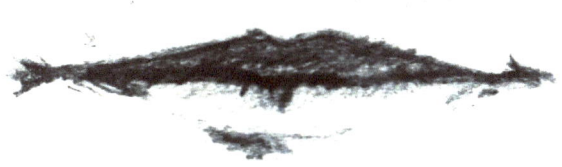

Graphic C

in a little shape of the upper gum. Don't draw all the teeth lines, even if you see them. They are too strong for the drawing. (see Graphic D - mouths below)

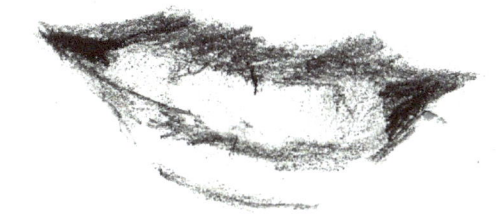

The roaming studio's step-by-step guide to drawing faces

Features Step-by-Step (Mouth)

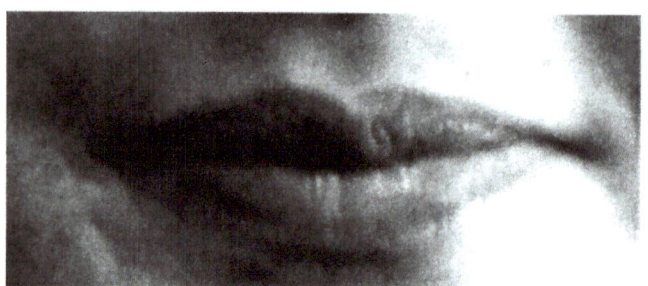

Step 1: Draw a dark, broken line marking the middle of the mouth

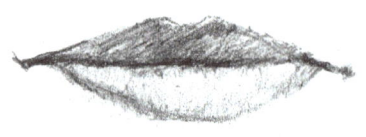

Step 2: Draw the top and bottom shape of the lips. Darken the top lip. Use medium to light tones for the bottom lip. Soften the dark middle line with your finger or the eraser.

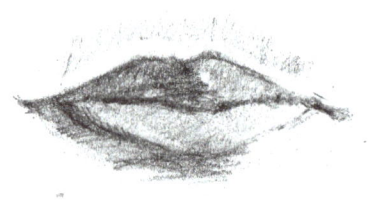

Step 3: Add a light area just above and running along the upper lip. Use eraser to lighten the bottom line of the lip, making it less distinct (there is a "lost edge", or similarity of lightness, or value, between one area and another).

EARS:

While we tend to make the eyes much larger than they really are (because that's what we focus on), we tend to make the ears on a person too small (because we aren't looking at them when we talk to someone). Mark out the top and bottom edges of the ears - the top is usually somewhere between the top of the eye and the eyebrow, and the bottom nearly lines up with the bottom of the nose, or sometimes goes even a titch lower).
(See graphic A - ears below)

Shade them, unless the light is hitting them. Figure them in, even if you can't see them because they are hidden by hair.

And now to the most distinctively different feature of the face ...

EYEBROWS:

Surprised? Eyebrows are the number one most distinctive feature for each of us. Some are bushy, others tweezed, others quite arched over the eye crease, while still others sit right on top of it. (See graphic A - eyebrows below).

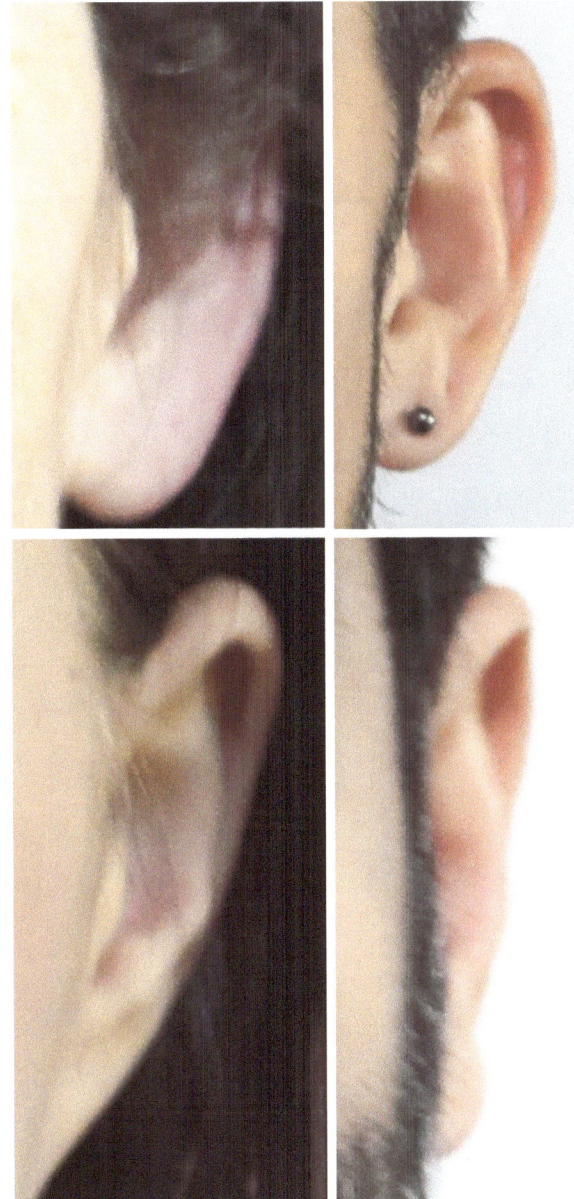

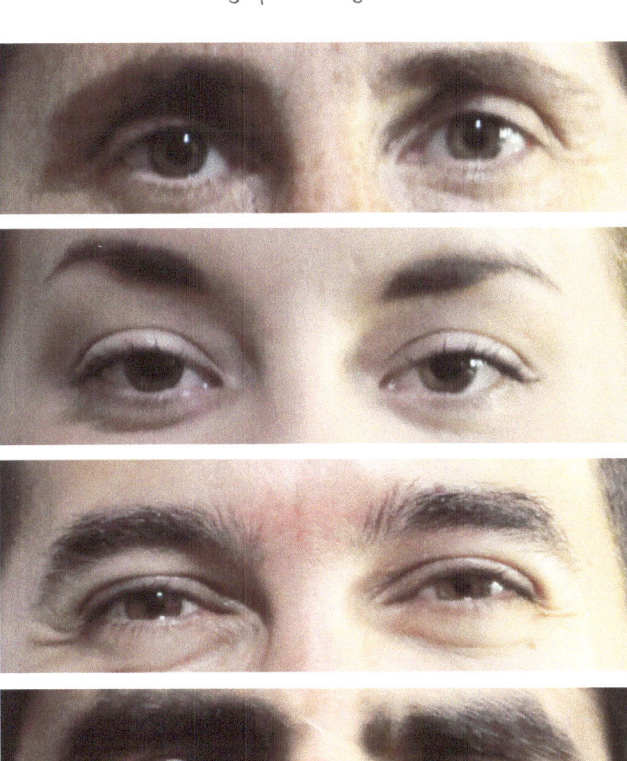

That's why we do them last, and we spend some time studying how they are shaped on the face. Notice where they start - lined up with the tear duct - and how they arch up, and then down, at the end near the ear. (thats because they are moving onto a different side, or plane, of the face). And remember, the eyebrows are dark towards the center, but they have soft edges as as they CURVE towards the outer side of the face.

PENCIL DRAWING STEP BY STEP

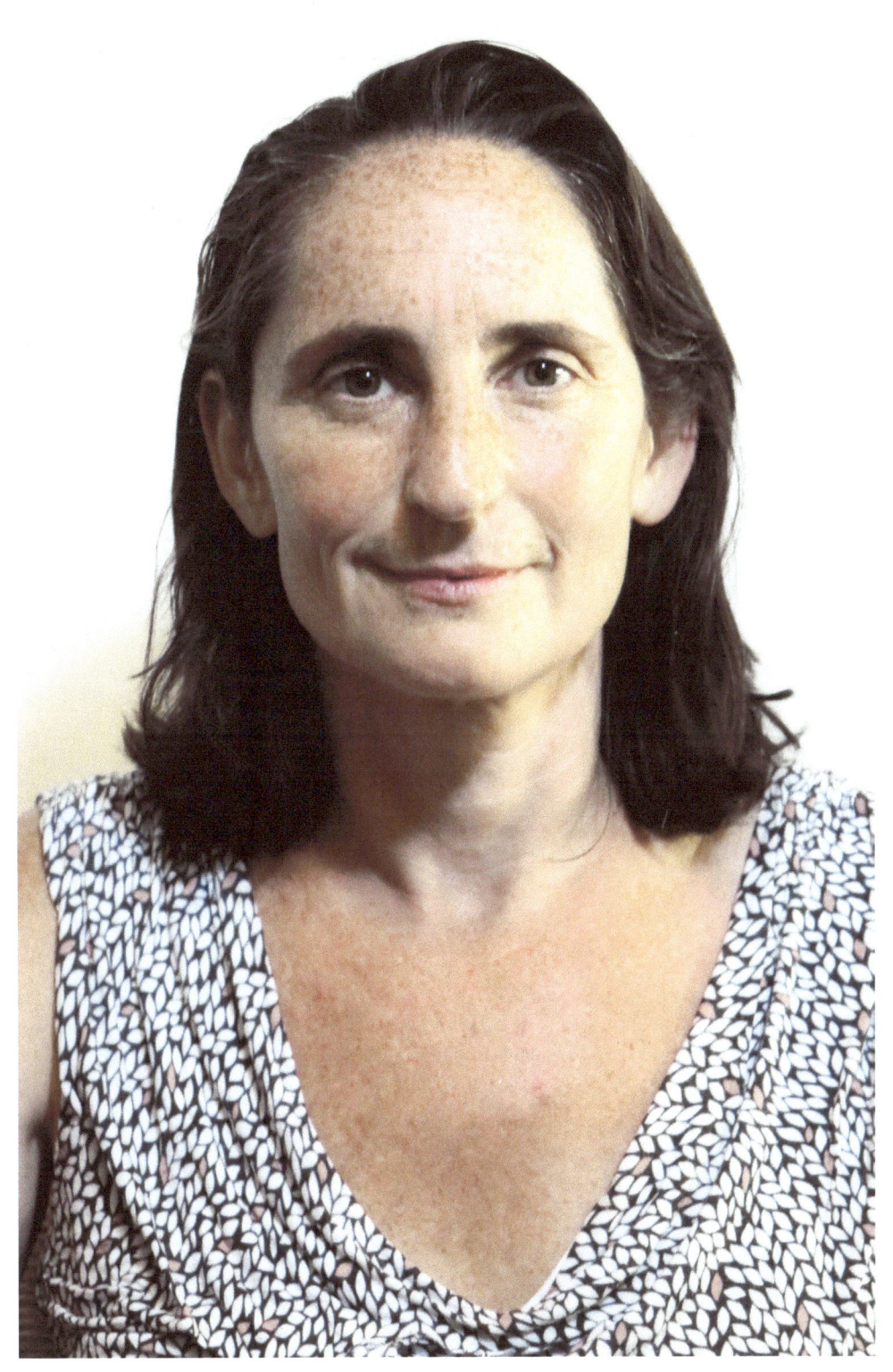

PENCIL DRAWING STEP BY STEP

Materials needed: HB Pencil and 2B or 4B pencil; sharpener; big eraser; drawing paper; ruler; copy of the photo on which this exercise is based.

Before you begin

... remember, drawing is fundamentally an exercise in construction. We are going to map out our blueprint, generally, before any significant details are added. You may want to launch in there and start on the eyes, but wait until you know where the eyes ARE (makes logical sense, right?). With that idea in mind, we'll start drawing not on our blank paper, but first on our source photo, as you see below:

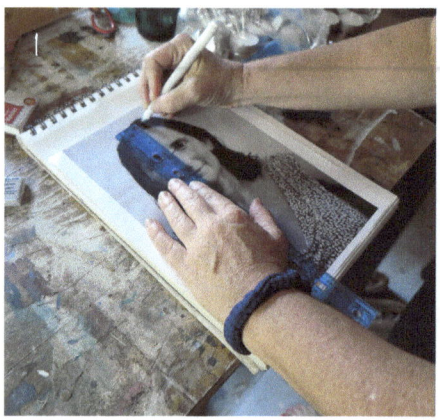
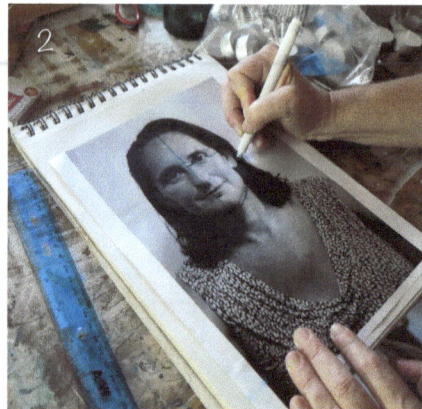
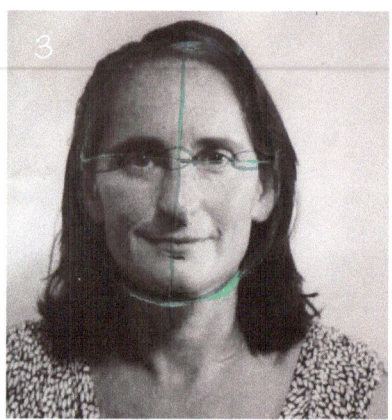

Steps 1-3

Sketch in the basic map of the face, as pictured on page 10, with a marker, pastel, or something that shows through on the copy. Start with your egg shape around the head (remember, this starts a little over the top of the hairline to include some, though usually not all, of the hair, and down around the outside edge of each ear. Note what is included in this shape - the entire face and the hair up to the edge of the ears - and what is not - the hair that poofs up above the top of the skull, the hair on the outside edges of the ear). Allow the shape to balloon out along the lower jawline, don't try to shape that yet.

Use your straight edge to draw a line straight down the middle of this egg shape. Find the halfway point (it should be at the middle of the eye line). Mark it with a small straight line. Find the halfway point between the eyeline and the base of the chin (it should be the bottom, or just below the bottom, of the nose), and mark it. Find the halfway point between the bottom of the nose and the chin (it should be the bottom, or near the bottom, of the lower lip). Mark it.

Draw a straight line with your ruler horizontally, through the middle of the eyeline (the center point), from the tip of one ear to the tip of the other. Measure the eye lengths. Note there should be one eye length on either side of the eye, and one in between the two. You may sketch them in if you like.

> **TIP:** If your features don't exactly sit on these marked points, either adjust your top line, or note where the features sit in relation to this point. They should be close! Some people's features are slightly elongated, so the chin might drop a little lower, or the nose might be a touch higher. But mostly, this is an unnatural elongation of the photo itself. (see Before you Begin, tips on taking selfies).

The roaming studio's step-by-step guide to drawing faces

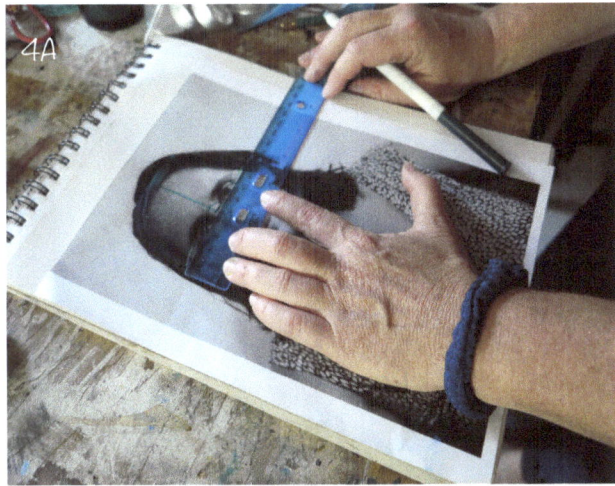
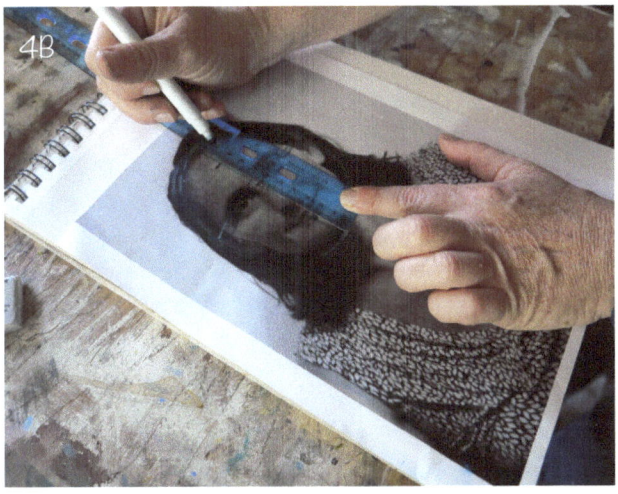
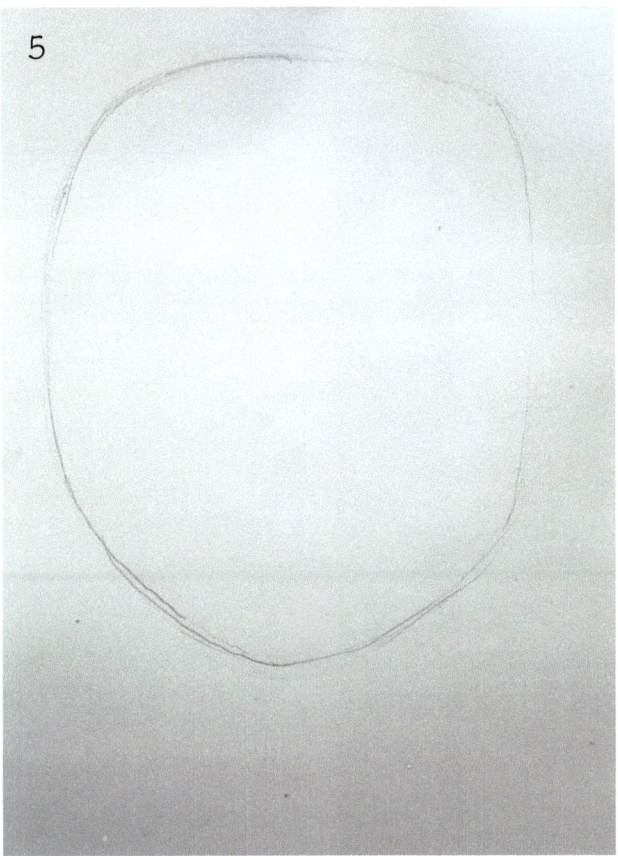

Step 4 (a and b)

This is a key measurement, and one that is often missed. Take your ruler, and measure the distance of the horizontal eyeline, from the tip of each ear. Place your ruler at the bottom of the chin, and note how high up the line goes (it's usually near the center of the forehead). If you like, mark the halfway point between the top of your egg shape and the eyeline, the top of the horizontal distance should hover around that mark, either above or below it. We will use this measurement to check out proportions later, when we draw our sketch on the paper.

Ok, finally, we are ready to begin drawing.

Step 5:

Start by drawing a basic egg shape to fit the page. Use light lines with your HB pencil that can easily be erased, nothing too heavy. And make this shape fit the page, whether you are working big or small (please don't try to transfer this drawing in its exact size to your drawing, using a ruler. Work as big as the paper allows. You will learn how these proportions will scale up or down with your drawing).

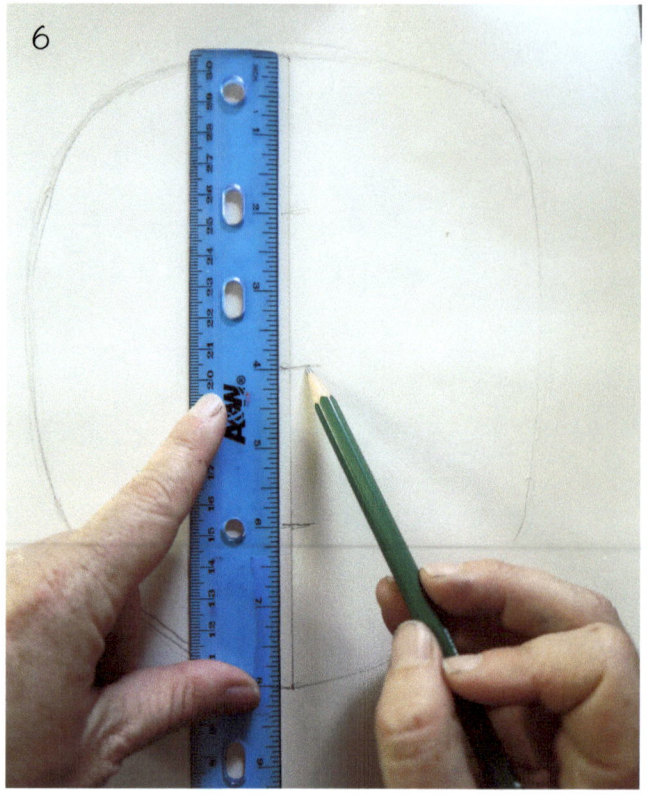

Step 6:

Draw a straight line down the middle of your egg shape, and use your ruler to find the same points we marked on this line in the drawing (the eyeline, bottom of the nose line, bottom of the mouth line). Draw a straight line horizontally from the middle eyeline, all the way across the face. Curve it up on each side, but only slightly. This line is primarily straight.

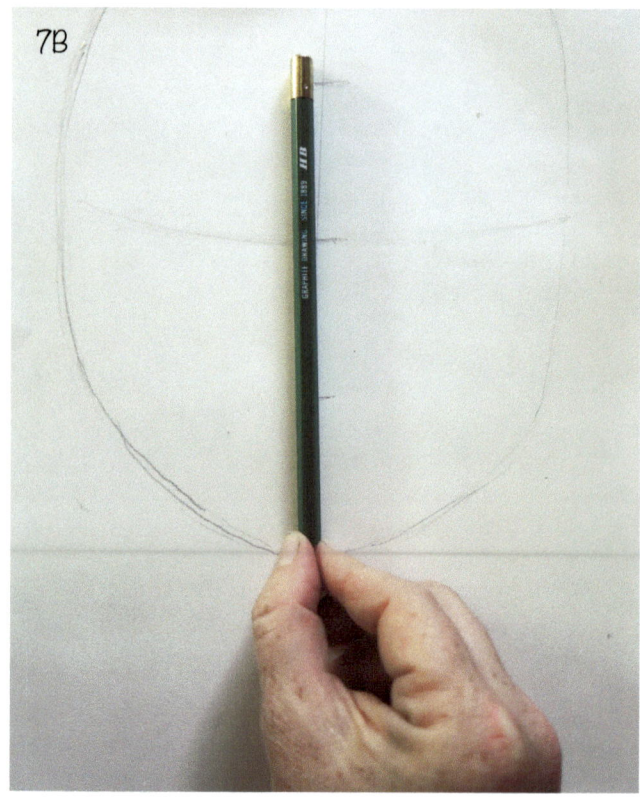

Step 7

(a and b): Now, check and see that your horizontal eye line is proportional. Do this by measuring the horizontal line (you can see I'm using a pencil here), and the lining it up with the vertical line, starting with the chin. Refer to step 4 to see if the horizontal crosses the vertical at about the same place on the head.

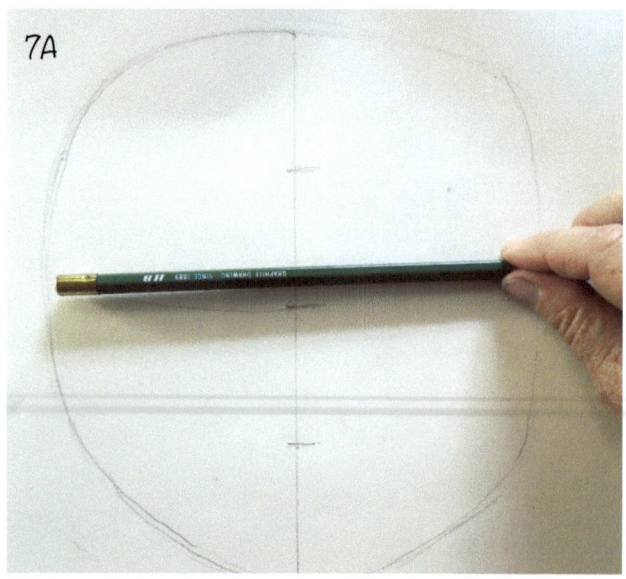

TIP: Some people get overwhelmed here, because we are going from straight measuring to estimating based on where things are located on the face. If you need to, add other markers (such as the halfway point between the top of the egg shape and the middle line). This is the key to drawing, and as you master it, you will see that regardless of the size, if your proportions are the same, your drawing will scale up and down easily.

The roaming studio's step-by-step guide to drawing faces

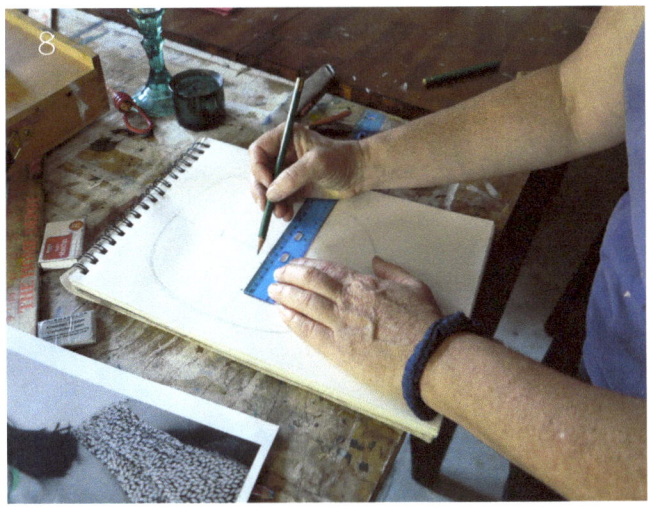

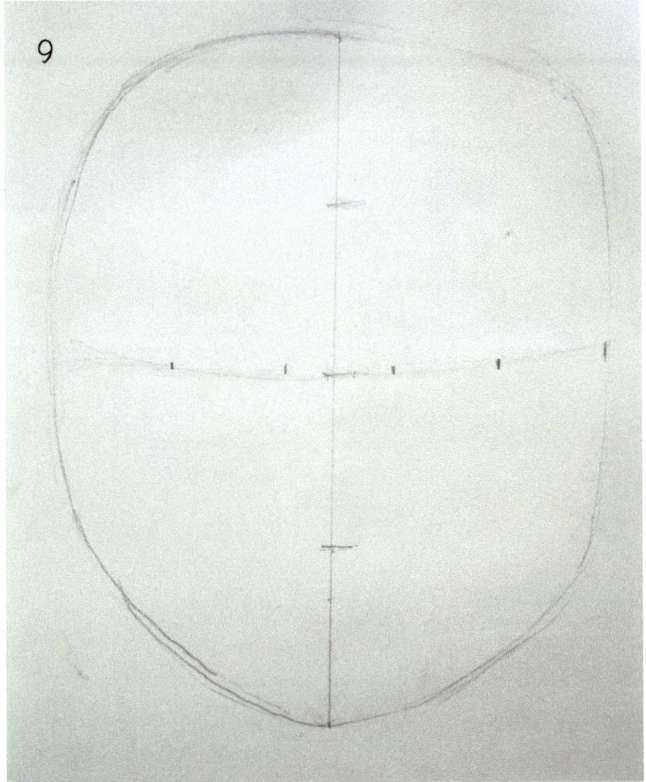

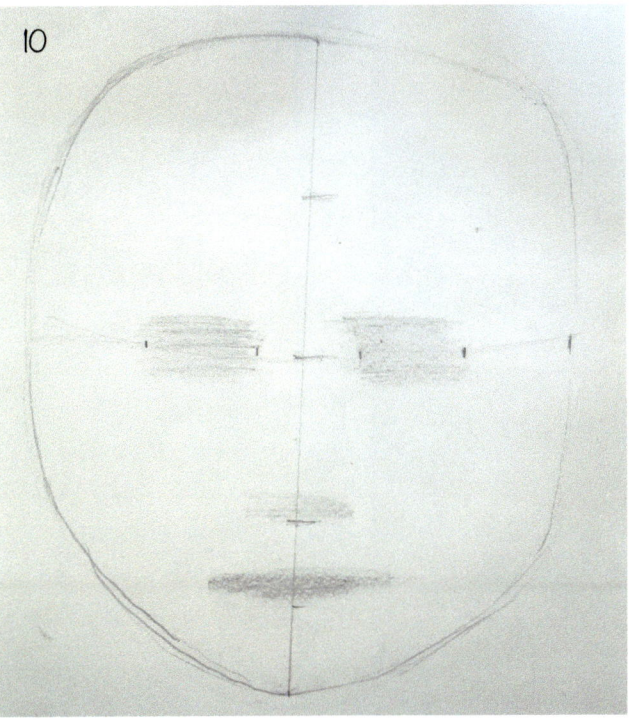

Step 10
Softly, with the side of your pencil, darken the areas around the eyes, and the bottom of the nose, and the mouth.

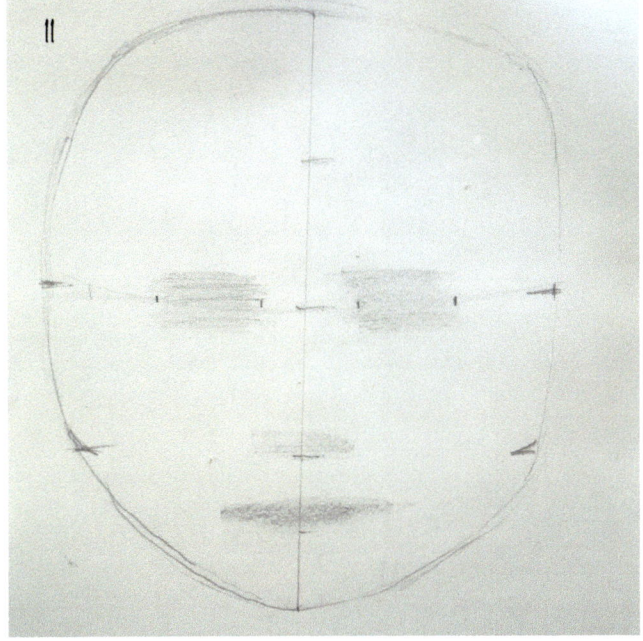

Step 8-9
Measure with your ruler or pencil across the horizontal line, and break it down into five equal sections. The middle two will be your eye location.

Step 11
Mark out the top and bottom of each ear (remember to stay inside your egg shape).

The roaming studio's step-by-step guide to drawing faces

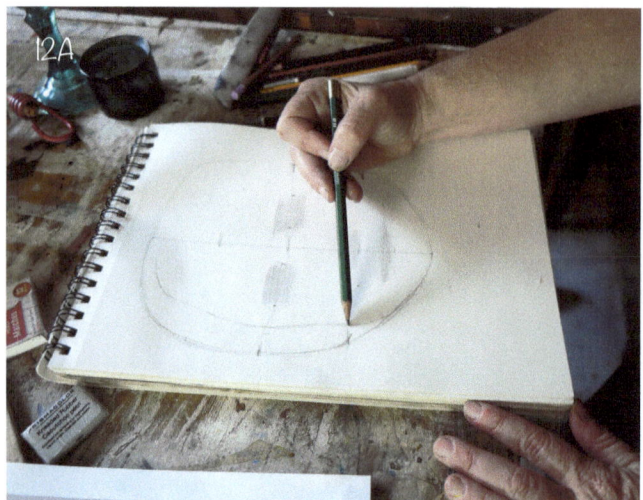

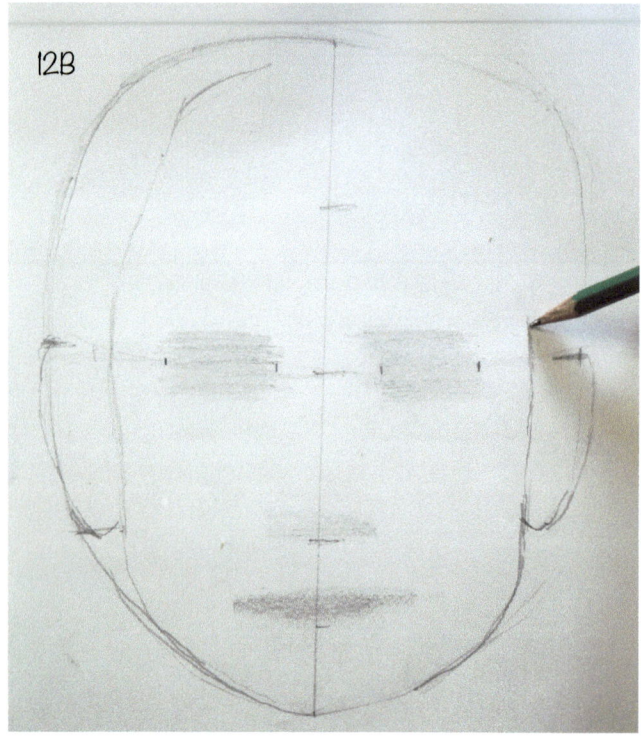

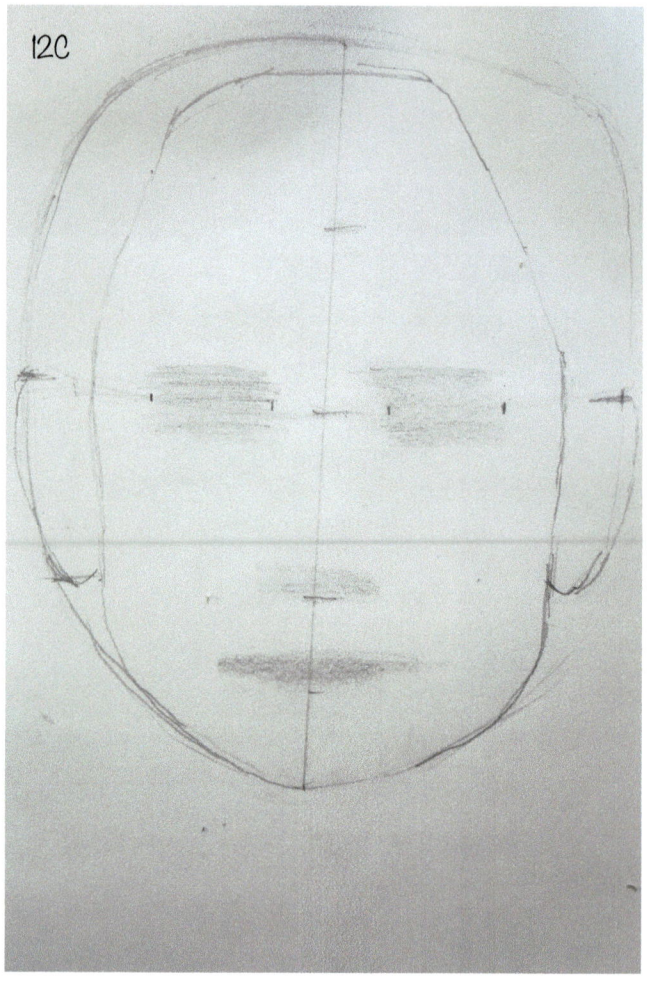

Step 12

(a-c) Now, start to sketch out the inside shapes of the jawline, the ears, and the hairline. Near the eyeline, the skin of the face usually takes up half an eye, and the hairline and ear, the other half. Continue working within the egg shape.

The roaming studio's step-by-step guide to drawing faces

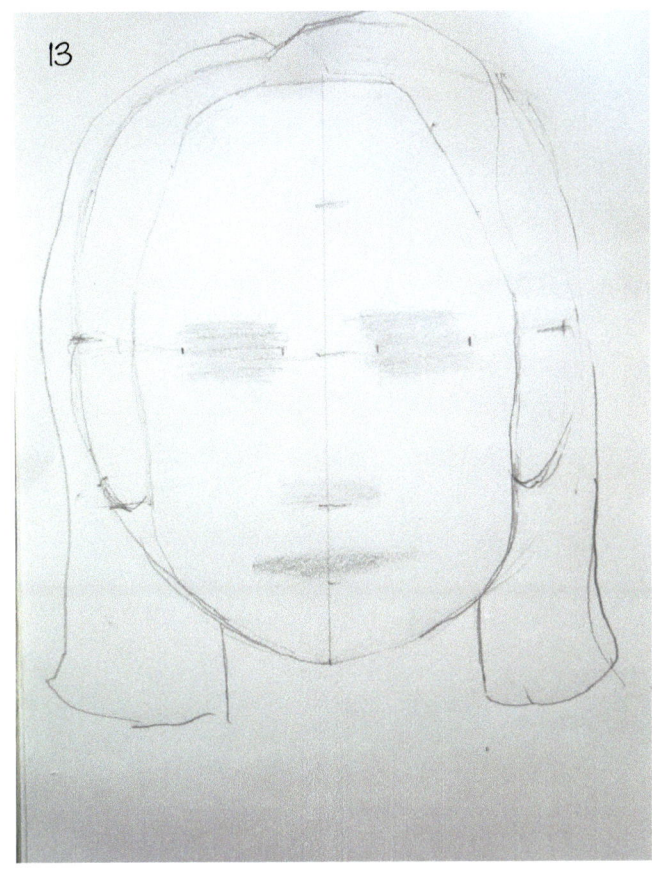

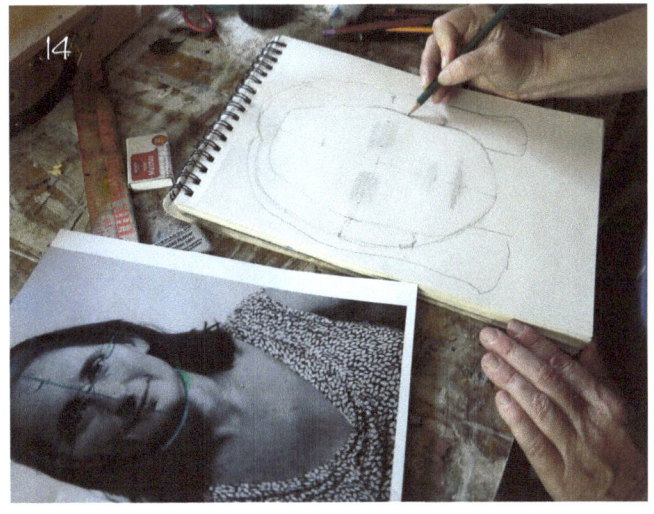

Step 14

Make adjustments to the outside shapes. You may notice that the jawline isn't shaped quite correctly, or the ears aren't down low enough, or any number of things that aren't perfect. Good! Professional artists learn to spend hours combing over their drawings, making small corrections as they go. You can't correct what you can't see!

Step 13

Once you finish, work on the shapes that lie outside the egg shape. Still focus on contour shapes, don't try to draw every hair, for example. Some hair shapes usually flop above the top of the egg shape. For long-haired people, the shapes come over the outer edge of the ear, and bounce down onto the shoulders, or below. For short-haired people, look at how the hairline above the ear lines up with the ear.

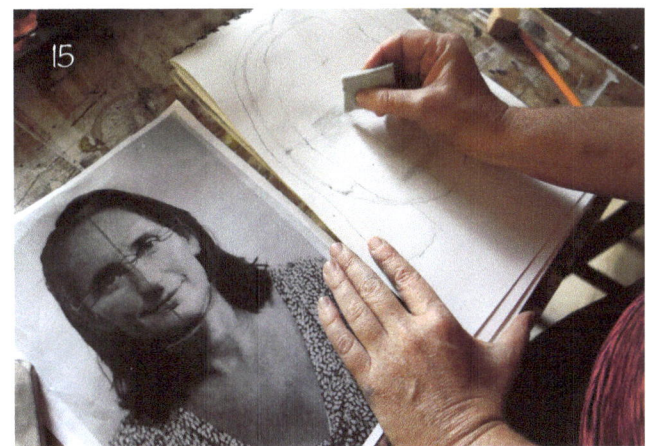

Step 15

When starting to add detail to the features, we want to avoid hard lines as much as possible. There are virtually none in the face, it's all soft edges of darks, mediums and lights. So it's natural, since we blackened the area where the features lie, that we'd start not with a pencil, but an eraser, to pull out the lights, as shown here with the eyes.

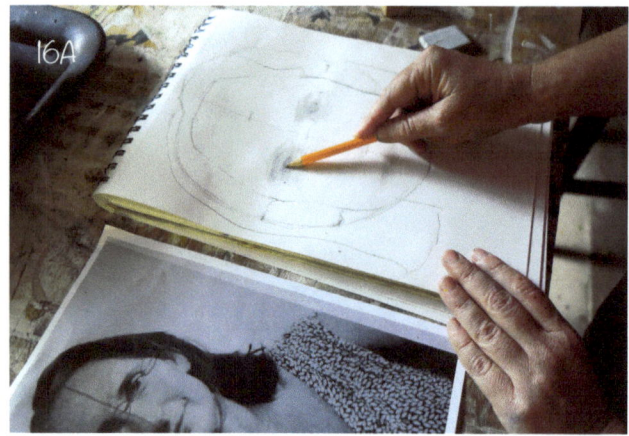

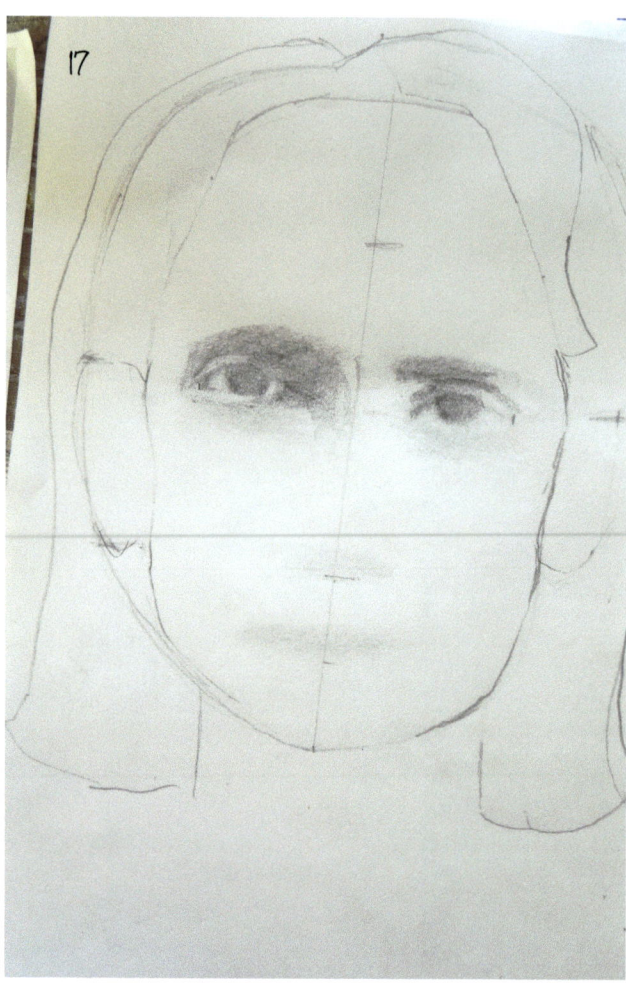

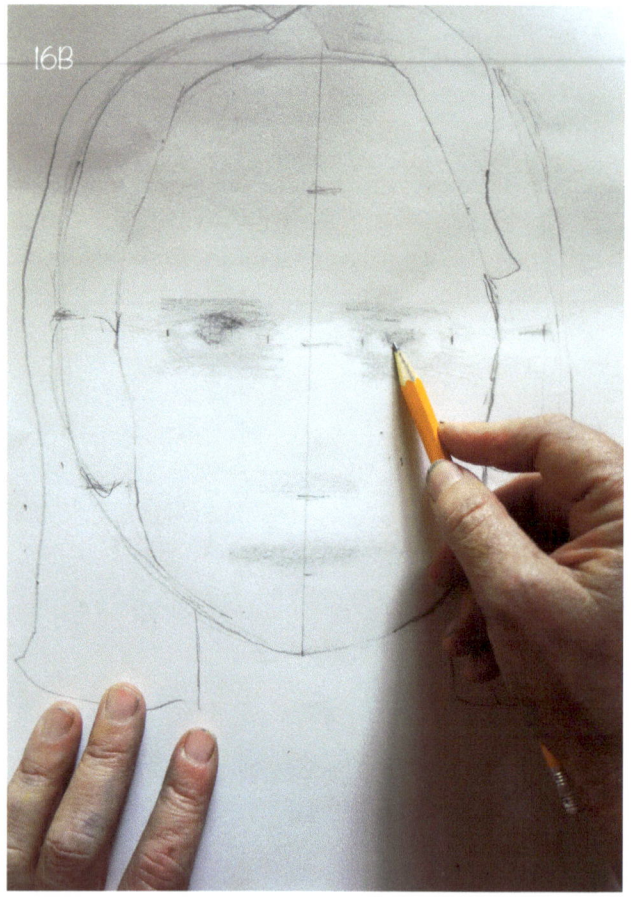

Step 17
As the eyes are roughed in, notice how there are lost edges - along the upper lid, for example, and the eyebrow on the left (or dark) side of the face. See how soft everything is. Note there is no dark line at the bottom of the eye, it's a light area pulled out by the eraser. We haven't added eye details yet - no bright highlight, no darkened iris edge or pupil yet. We are still working on the outer, bigger, light and dark shapes.

Step 16a and b
Once the whites are established, and the pencil is introduced, note I'm using it on its side, not the pointed tip. As I'm darkening and lightening the areas around the eyes, I'm trying to avoid those strong, hard lines.

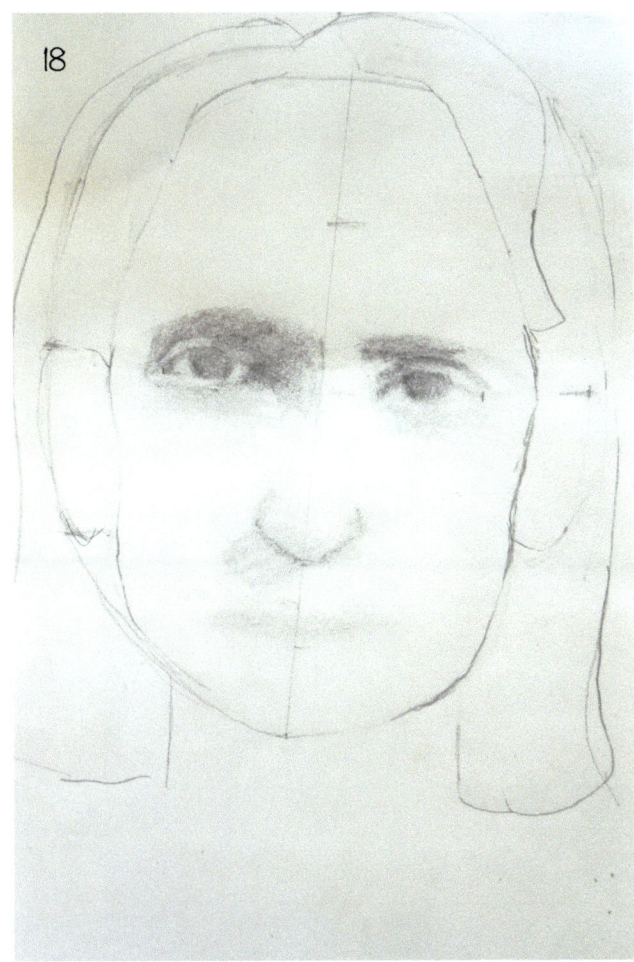
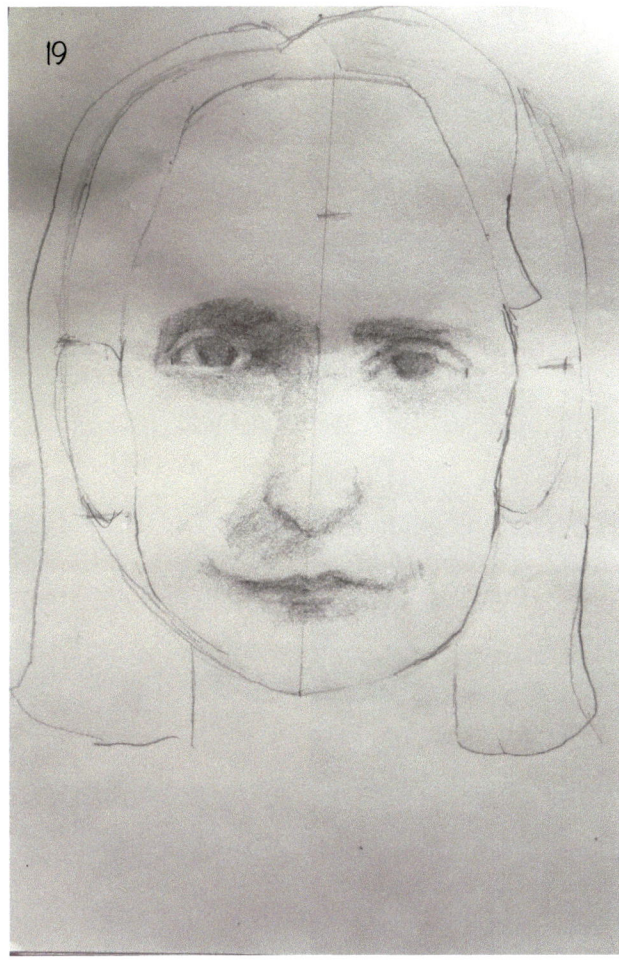

Step 18

Similarly with the eyes, fewer lines are more with the nose. This person is a fox, meaning the nostrils ride a little higher than the bottom of the nose. Sketch in the outline of the bottom shape, and the nostril edges, but it's still soft. Remember to line up the nostrils with the pink triangle at the inside edge of each eye. I've also roughed in the shadow under the nose leaning to the left.

Step 19

I started with the dark middle line, which extends, remember, to roughly line up the middle of each iris. This is still soft. Still using the edge of my hB pencil, rather than the tip. Sketch in the top lip, which is darker than the bottom lip. Bottom lip on the right side is another lost edge, this time to the light side, so don't complete the bottom line.

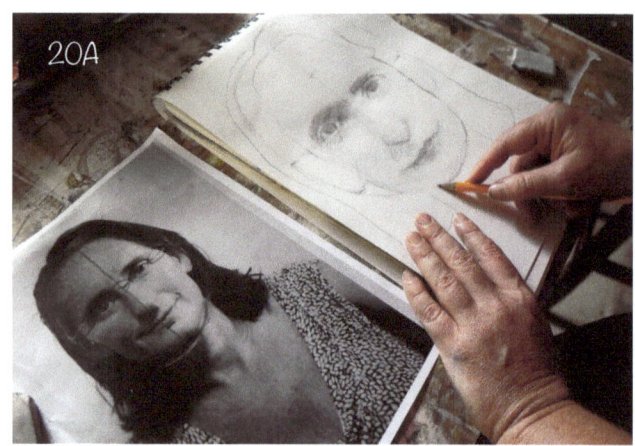

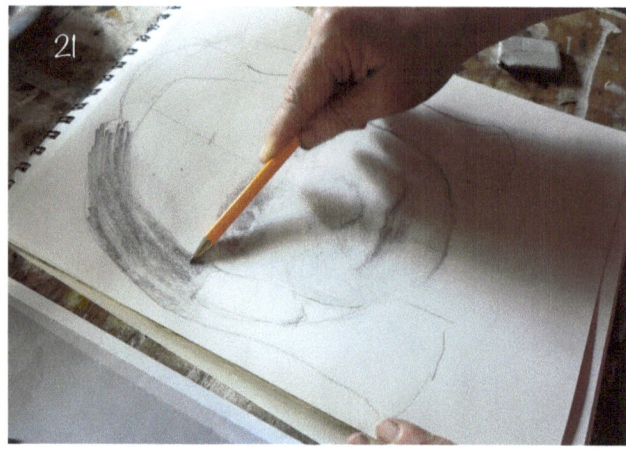

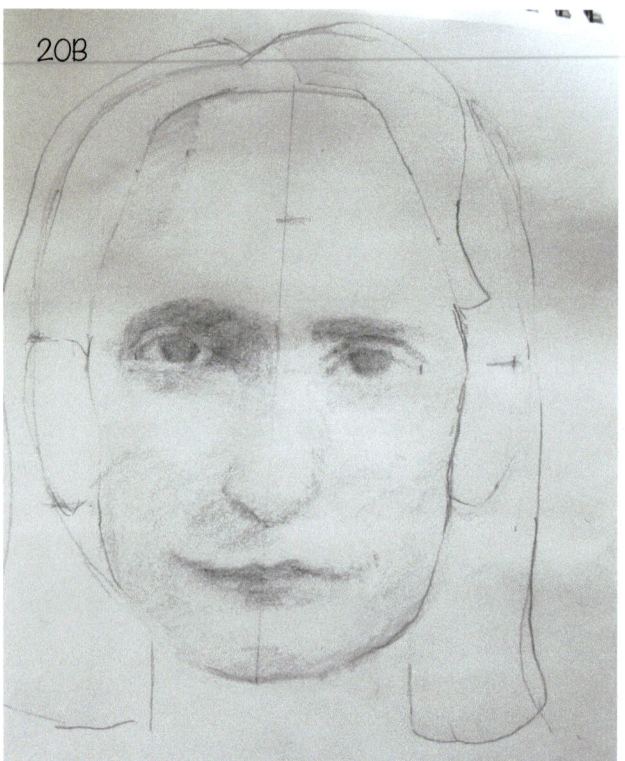

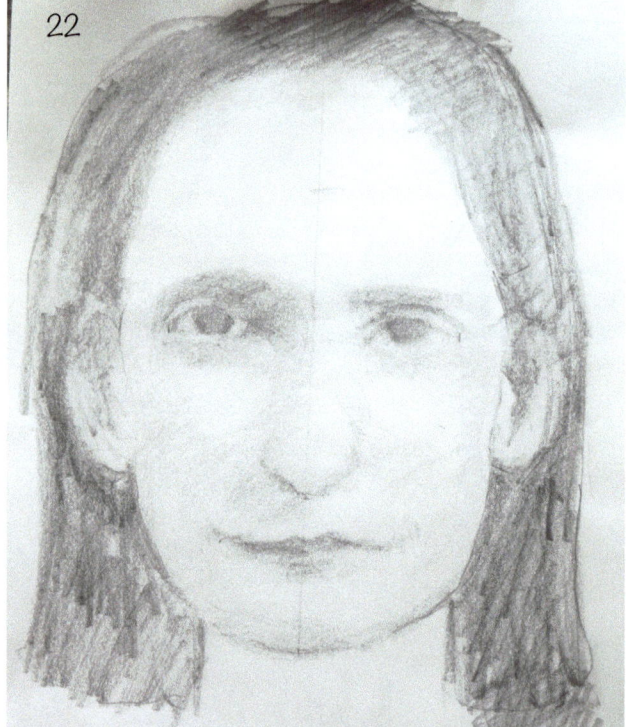

Step 21
Don't draw each individual hair! Note that the hair is a series of dark, and lighter masses. But mostly dark, especially where it meets skin (99 percent of the time). Note how strongly I'm darkening the hair.

Step 20a and b
I begin adding the shading - referring to the shading guide on page 12 - still using my pencil edge. The whole bottom of the face is darker than the top. Note that on the dark side of the face each of the different planes is slightly darker than on the equivalent planes on the right side of the face.

Step 22
I add in the neck (note where the neck lines line up with features of the face) and continue darkening the hair

The roaming studio's step-by-step guide to drawing faces

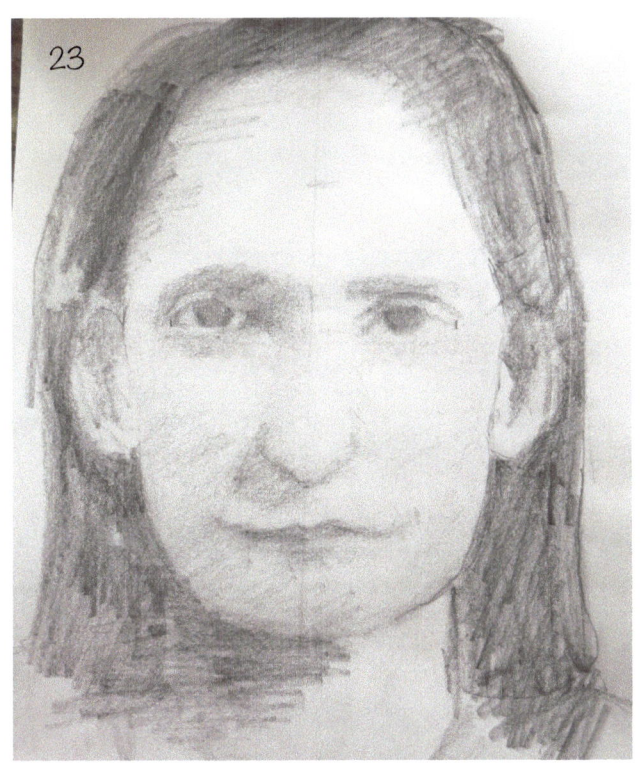
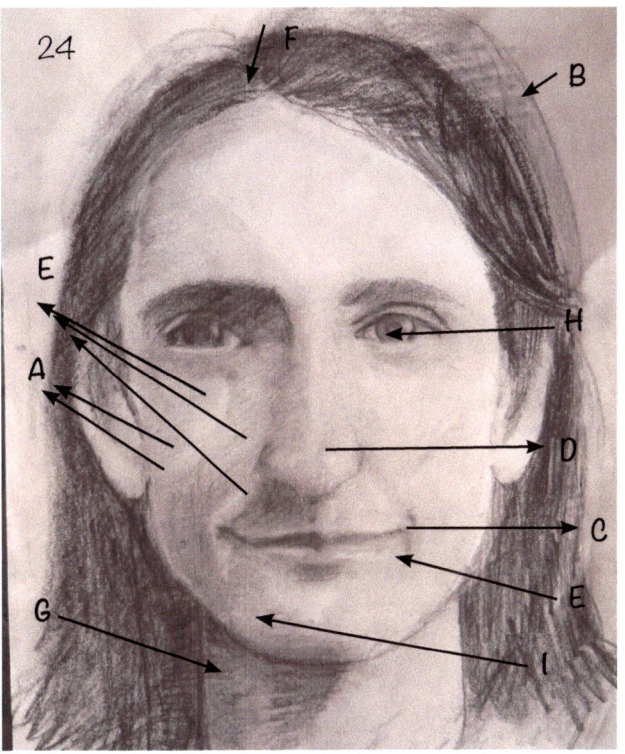

Step 23
Now I add in the darker shading on the face, add the neckline, and darken the hair with a 4B pencil.

Step 24
Once you've laid out the base outer construction, finally, now it is time to focus on the details that make each face different. There is a lot of back and forth happening, and a lot of erasing. This is normal artistic process, don't be discouraged, it means things are going well! Some details of my final portrait:

A. Darkened shaded areas, particularly on portrait dark side
B. Pulled hairline down, reshaped it, both outside and where hairline meets skin, reducing size of forehead
C. Reshaped mouth - I had to do this three times!
D. Reshaped nose, lessening the angle of the bottom lines significantly. I also shaded the bottom of the nose, blending that into the shadow under the nose
E. Reshaped jaw line on both sides, making it more square
F. Darkened hair, evened out mark-making. Note hair is darkest where it meets skin.
G. Thinned the neck lines
H. Added eye details - darkened iris rim, darker iris on top, lighter on bottom, etc. (see page 15 for details)
I. Pulled out highlighted areas with eraser

STUDENT TRY PENCIL DRAWING

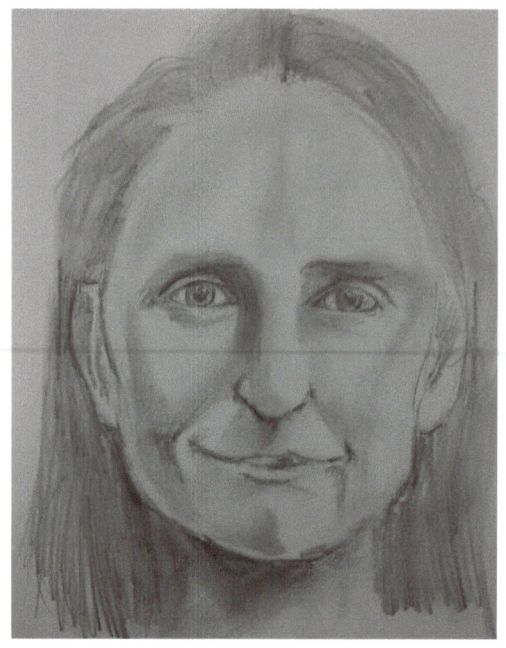

Katya Melluish, age 42

Leah's notes

I love Katya's drawing! She's paid great attention to the shapes and shadows around the eyes, the quirk of the mouth on one side for the smile, and the face shape. Shading is lovely, features are all in the right places. I adore the reflected light edge on the dark side. My only critique? The bottom of the nose shape extends just a millimeter further out, and the slant from the bottom tip towards the side nostril isn't quite as slanted as she's drawn it.

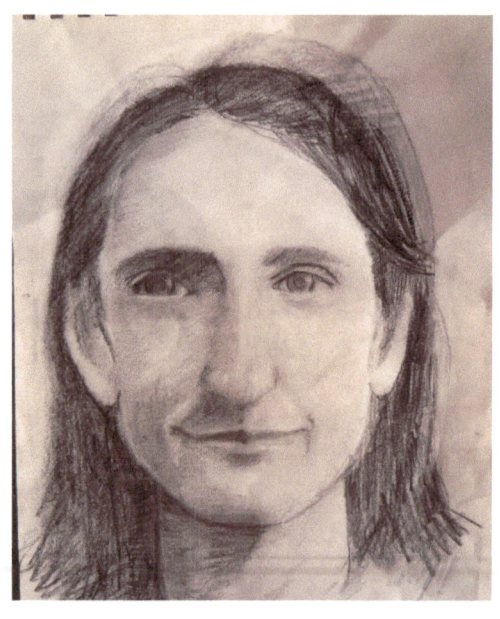

Leah's finished pencil drawing

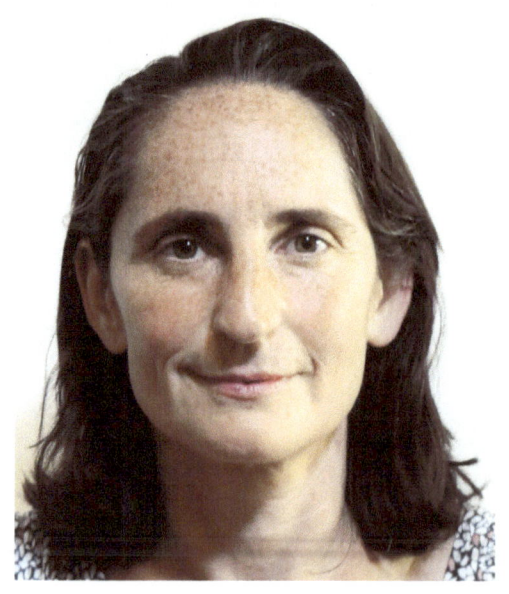

Leah's original portrait

TRY PENCIL DRAWING YOURSELF

Charcoal Drawing Step by Step

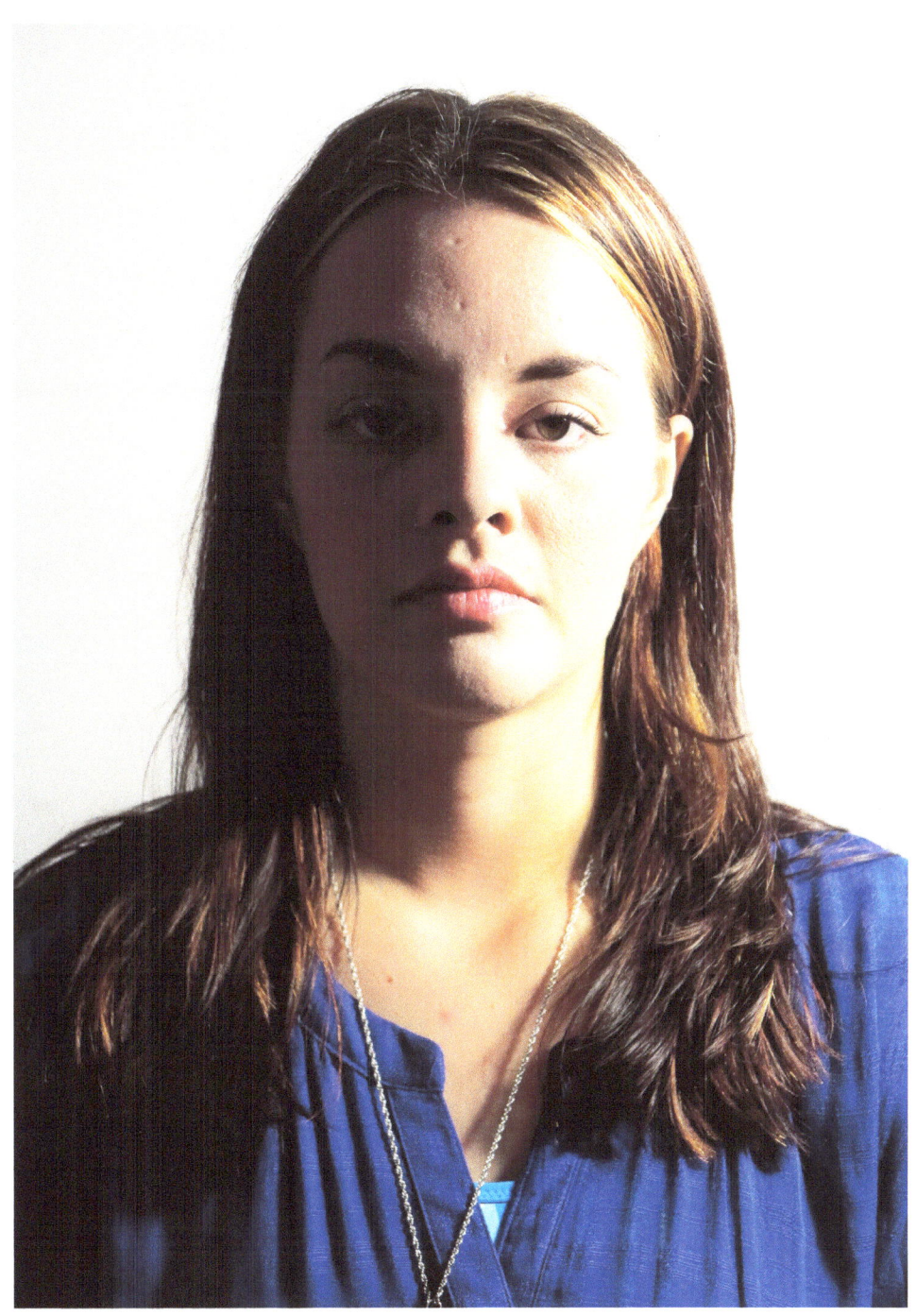

CHARCOAL DRAWING STEP BY STEP

Materials: A combination of vine, willow and student grade charcoal sticks (please AVOID compressed charcoal), newsprint paper, kneaded eraser, paper towels, copy of the source photo for this exercise, ruler

Before you begin ...

While drawing with the pencil is about finding the outer contour lines, and then working inwards, charcoal is about piecing together light and dark shapes (think jigsaw puzzle). We start by toning our paper to a medium dark hue, and then pulling out the lightest areas with an eraser, before starting in with the tip of the charcoal. For some, this will be easier than using a pencil, for others, more challenging. Allow this exercise to be either of those things for you. Just know that the pencil and charcoal need very different methods for recreating the face. Ultimately, with practice, you'll get better at both methods.

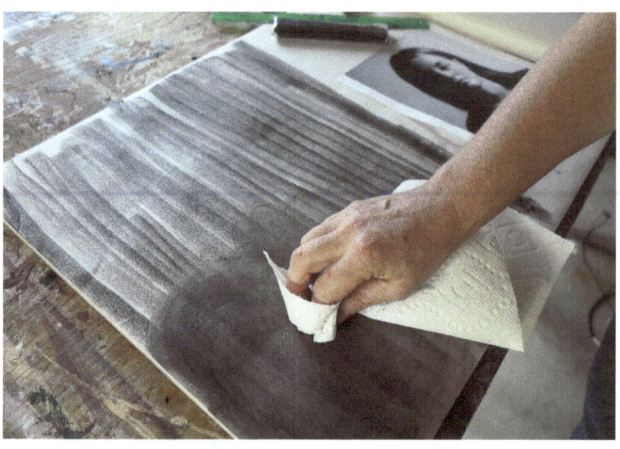

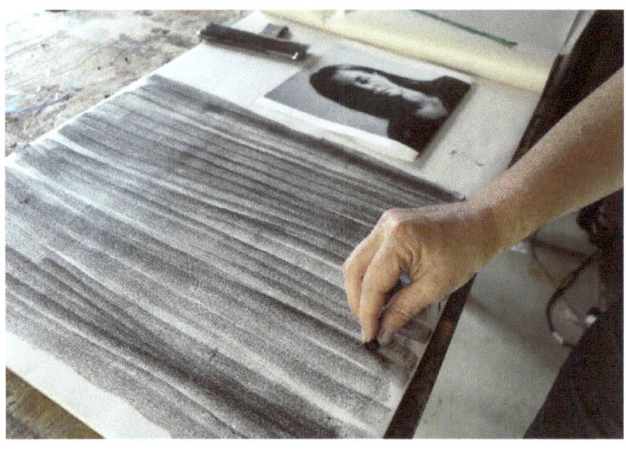

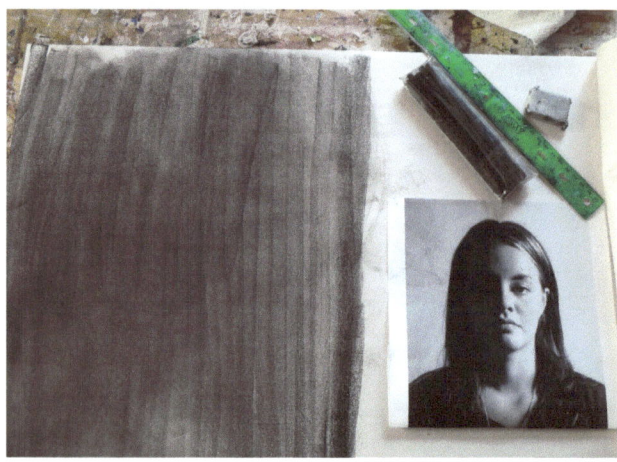

Step 1

Tone your paper by laying a charcoal stick on its side, and covering the entire paper with charcoal. If on a values scale of one to five, one is lightest and five is darkest, aim for a 3-4 value.

Step 2 (a and b)

Use a paper towel to smudge the toned paper so fewer charcoal lines show through, and the dark tone is smoothed

The roaming studio's step-by-step guide to drawing faces

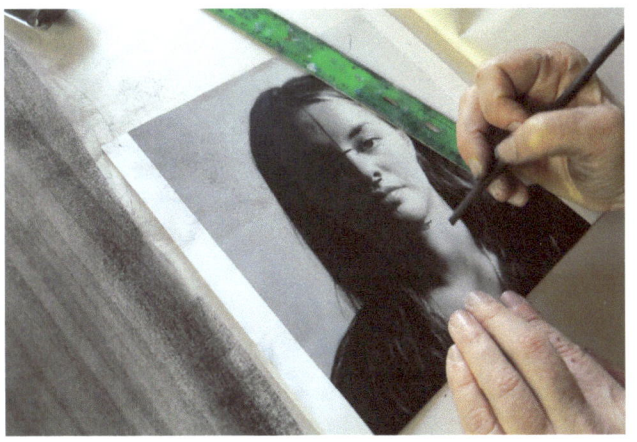

Step 3
Like you did with the pencil drawing, mark the major measurements on your photo source

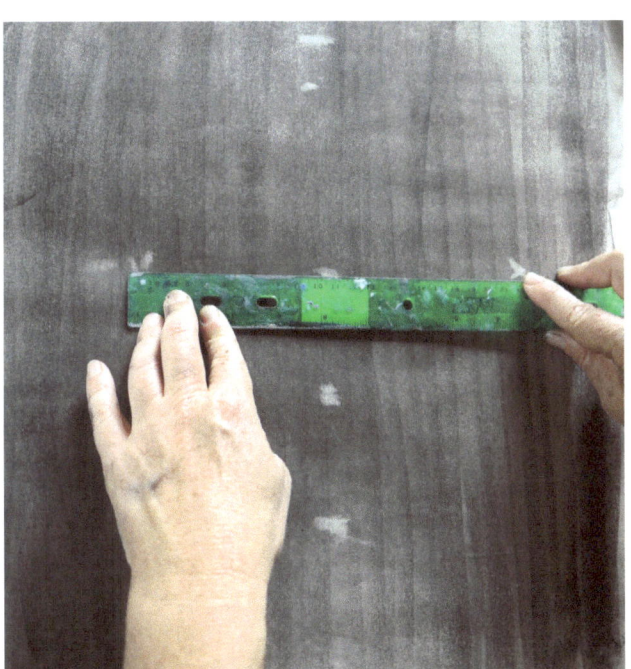

Step 4
Mark out those same measurements on your toned charcoal paper, using an eraser.

Step 5 (a and b)
Once you've marked out the proportions, still using the eraser, begin erasing out the lightest shapes on the face. This will be less about drawing in the outer lines, and more about seeing the light shapes within the face.

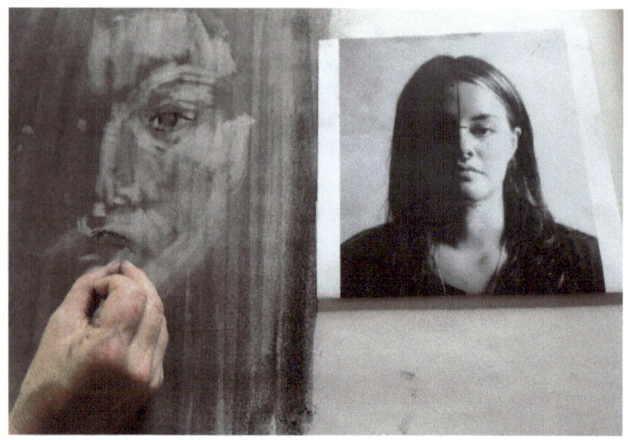

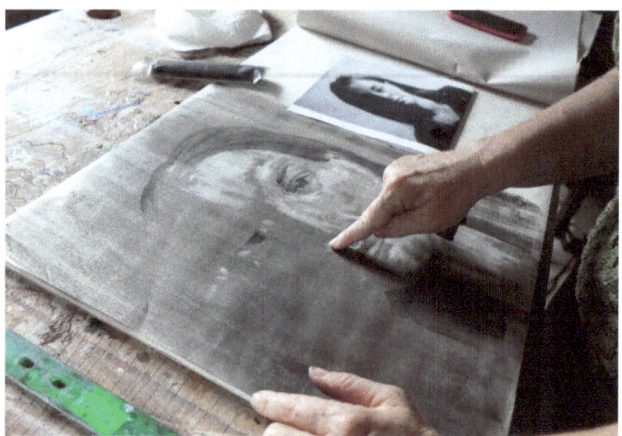

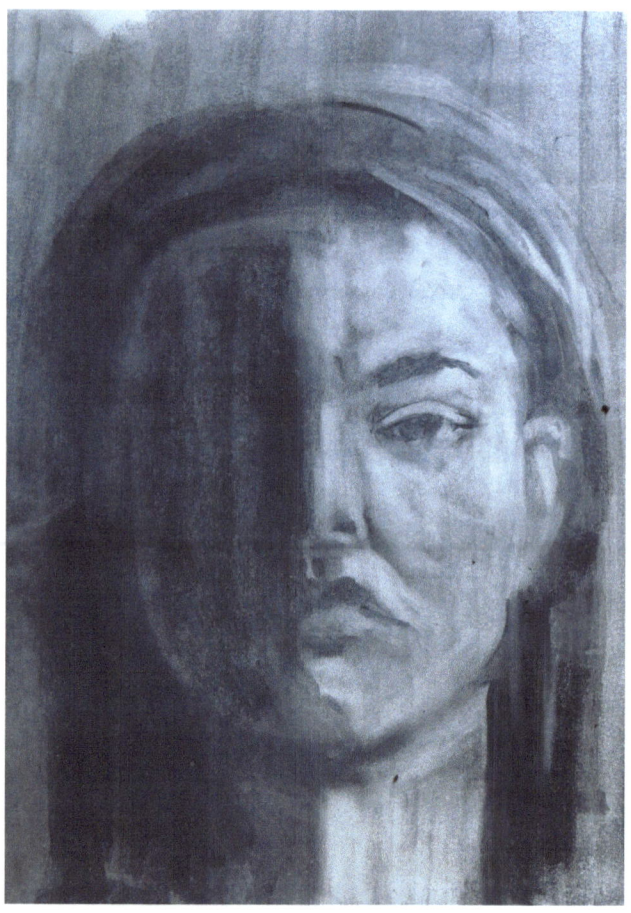

Step 6 (a and b)
Once you've got the lightest parts of the face, you can go in with different charcoal sticks to add in the darkest areas. Use your fingers, or the paper towel, to blend the surfaces and move things around.

Step 7
Work primarily with the light side (our right side), leaving the darker side untouched, except for pulling out a medium value line with your eraser along the outside edge of the dark side of the face, where the skin meets the hairline. This is called the reflected edge.

The roaming studio's step-by-step guide to drawing faces

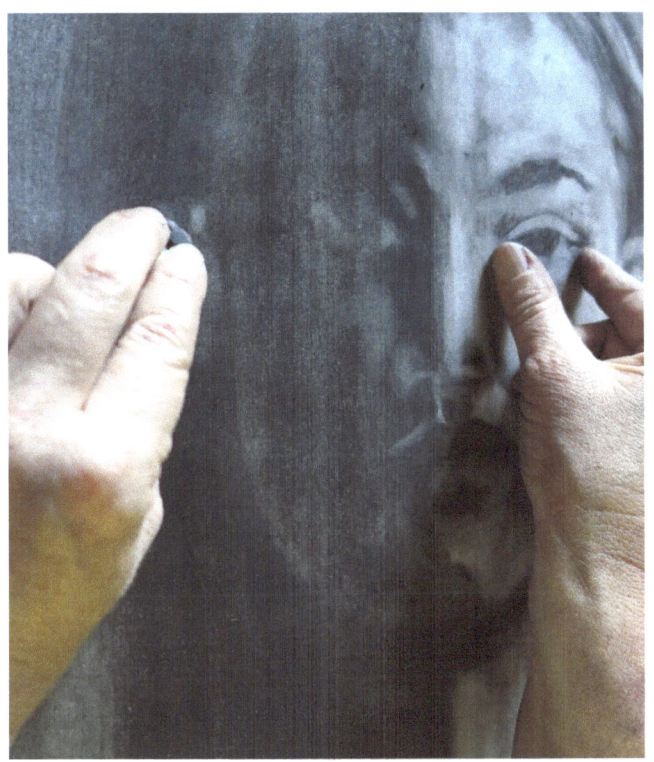
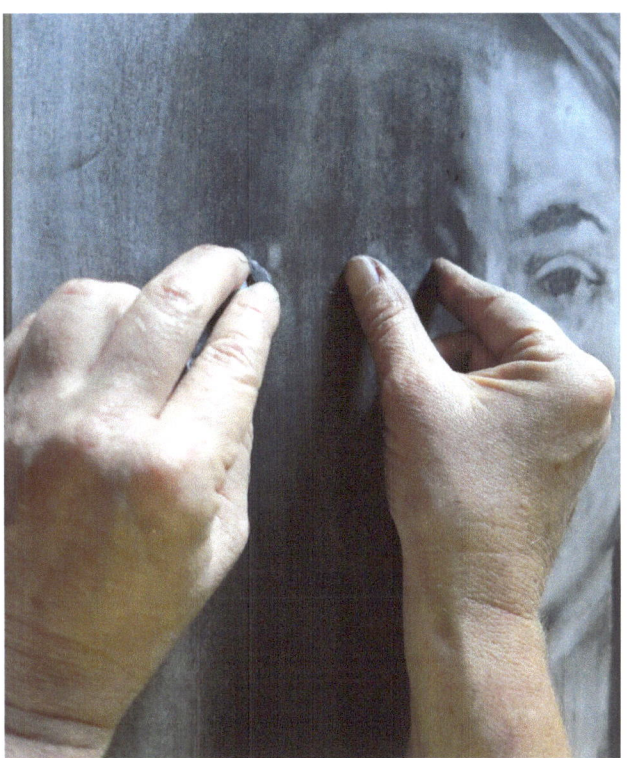

Step 8
The darker side of the face is so dramatically that, you'll only see hints of the lightest parts. Use your understanding of measurements and proportion to locate a hint of the whites of the eyes, side nostril lines, and a little bit of the cheek.

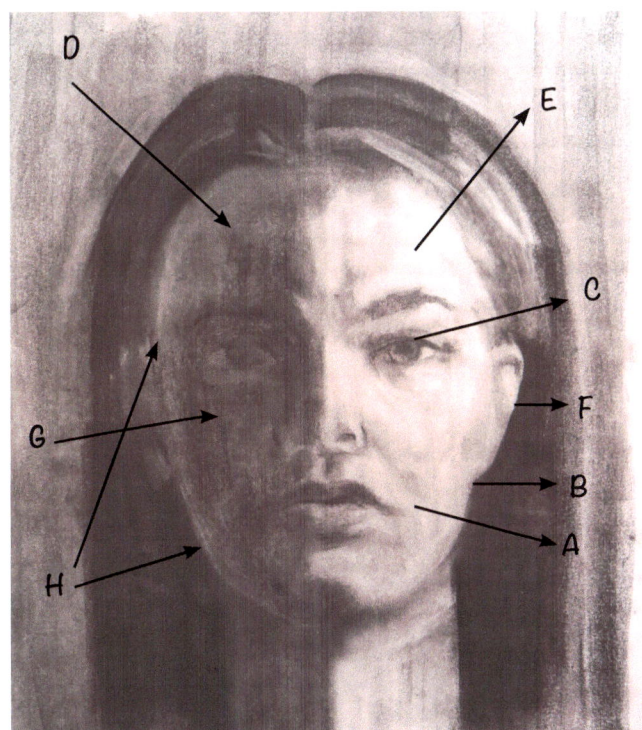

Step 9
A. Reshaped mouth, lessening the downward curve of top lip

B. Widened nose, pulling out shadow side with eraser

C. Darkened and reshaped upper lid, added eye details as described on page 15

D. Even out all shaded areas, using a finger or chamois

E. Even out out light areas with eraser

F. Reshaped ears, deepening the angle towards the head

G. Using eraser gently to indicate light areas in the shadowed side of the face

H. Reshaped jawline and forehead shape using reflected light

STUDENT - TRY CHARCOAL DRAWING

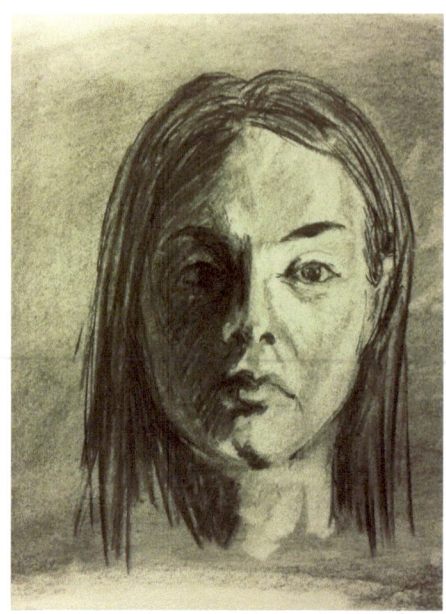

Katya Melluish, age 42

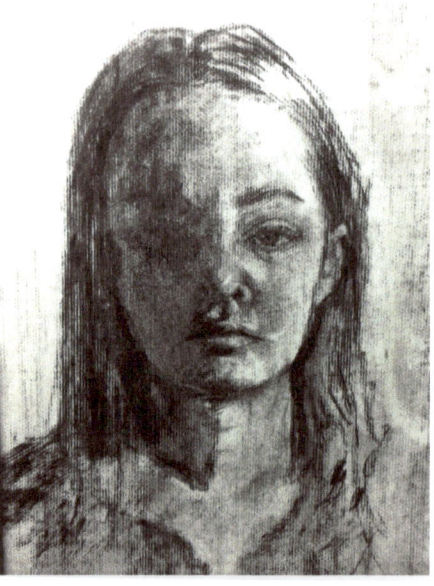

Nats Grant Logan, age 39

Leah's notes

What I like about these two examples is that both students went through the charcoal step-by-step lesson, but still wound up with unique results. These step by steps are a process that demonstrate a technique, but there is still room for individual expression. Natalie's drawing has more soft edges and her darks are darker, while Katya's drawing contains more strong contour lines. Both are effective methods for using charcoal.

I like how Natalie's drawing conveys the soft, dark mood of the photo, particularly in her masterful use of light on the top of the model's head and the neckline on the light side. She could improve her measurements to get more likeness - her eyes are slightly too big, and too far down the face - the eyebrows are where the middle of the eyeline should be. This gives the model a slightly odd-shaped look to her head.

Katya's measurements are solid, and I love how she's gotten the quirk of the eyebrow and shape of the eye on the light side. To improve this drawing, I'd tell her to darken the dark side of the face more, meaning some parts of the features should have lost edges in the shadows, and I'd like to see the hair filled in more solidly.

TRY A CHARCOAL DRAWING OF YOURSELF

INK DRAWING
STEP BY STEP

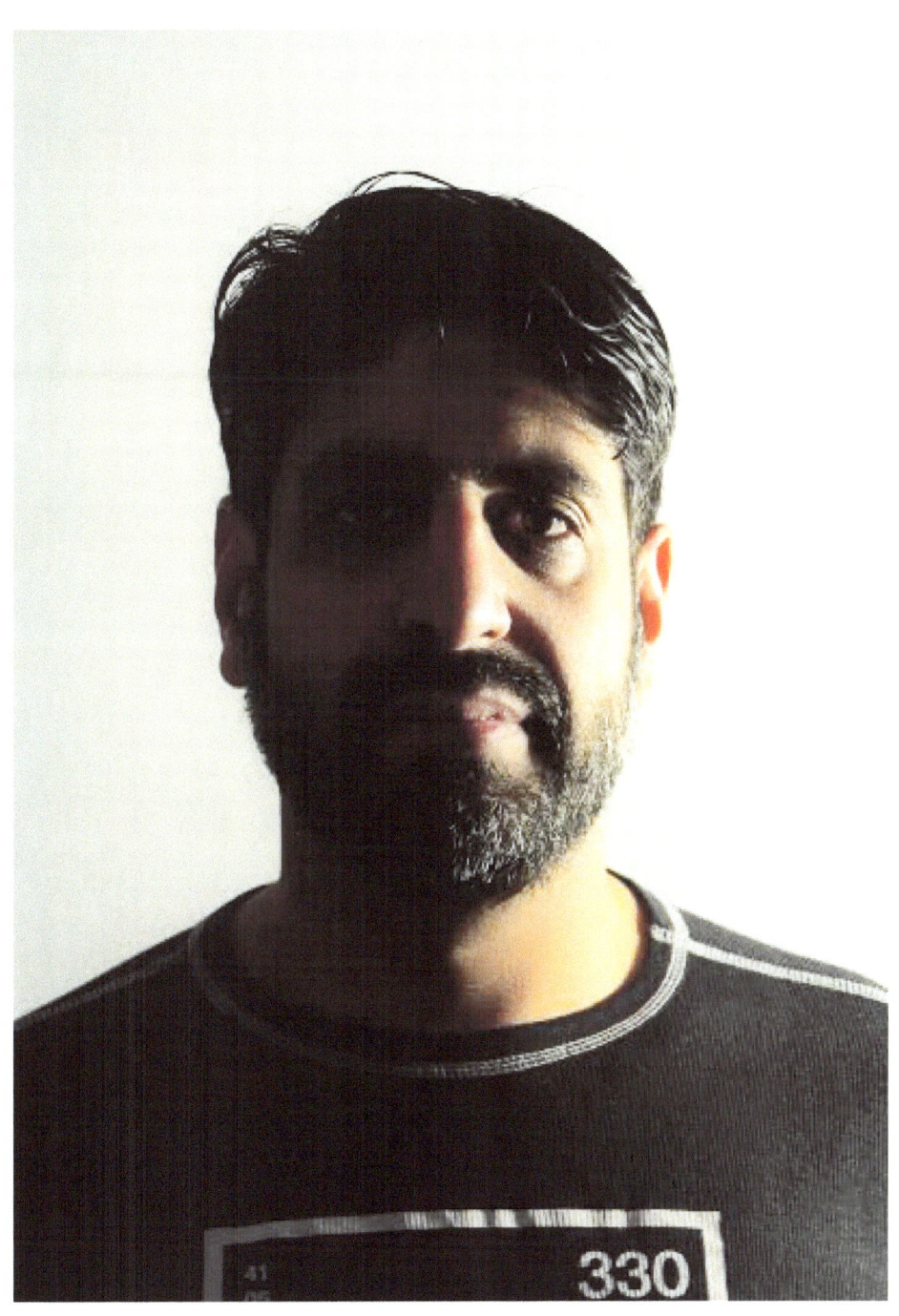

INK DRAWING STEP BY STEP

Materials: Bristol paper, bamboo brush, bamboo pen, paper towels, copy of the source photo for this exercise, ruler, one or two jars of water- for diluting the ink, paper for testing your marks

Before you begin ...

Ink scares us, because it feels so permanent. "I can't erase it," one thinks, and that's why it's so challenging. In fact, ink used this way - with a bamboo brush, pen, and starting with ink diluted with water - allows us to make our initial drawings first, and correct things later. Like charcoal, ink requires us to think in dark and light shapes, rather than contour lines. But instead of starting with the light shapes first, ink starts you off with the darkest shapes, using ink diluted with water and a brush. Once you are sure of the darker areas, you can layer in darker inks with less (or no) water. Mistakes can often be wiped off (while still wet) with a bit of towel. The bamboo pen is brought in only at the end to introduce the few contour lines of the face we need to see. Ink is fast, and will make you feel you are on a carnival ride! The challenge is to stay with it to the final changes, even when you think the drawing is wrong,

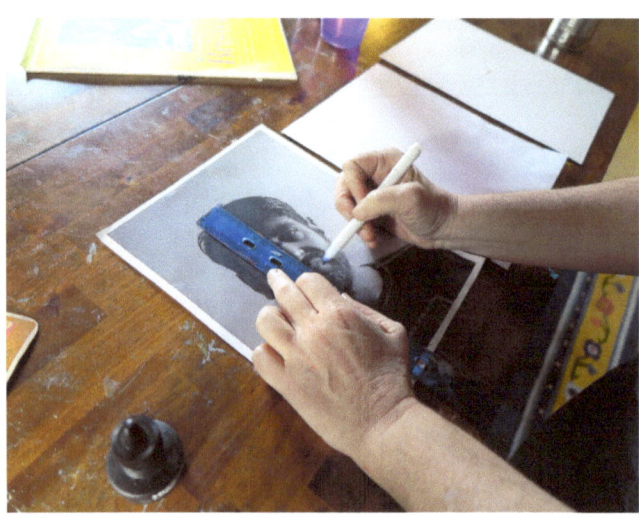 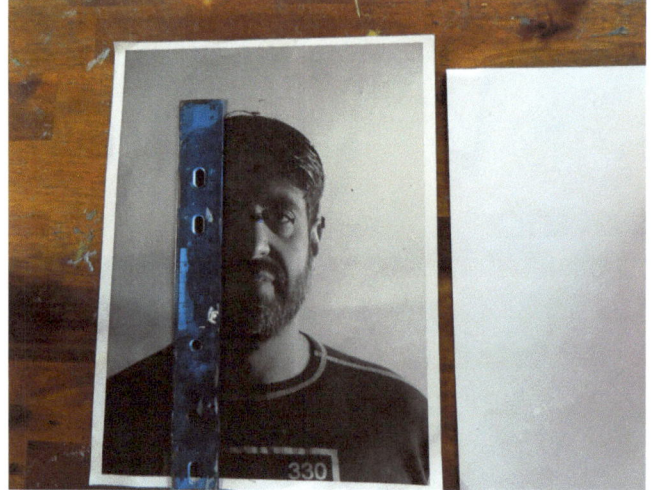

Step 1a, 1b

As with your other two subjects, draw a line down the center of your source face, mark the top of the head and the bottom of the chin, and find the halfway point on that line (the middle of the eye line). Find the halfway point between the eyeline and the chin, and you'll see the top of the lip (normally the bottom of the nose, but he's got his head tilted up slightly). The last halfway point, between the top of the lip and the chin, is located just below the bottom of the mouth. Note that, like all face forward subjects, this one is five equal eyes across from ear tip to ear tip.

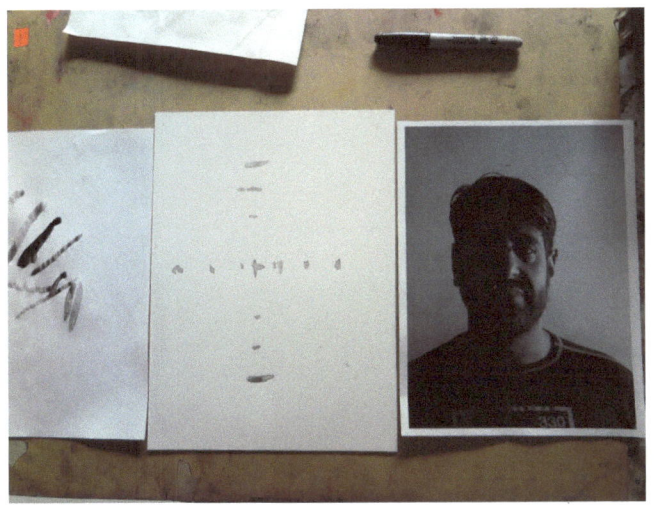
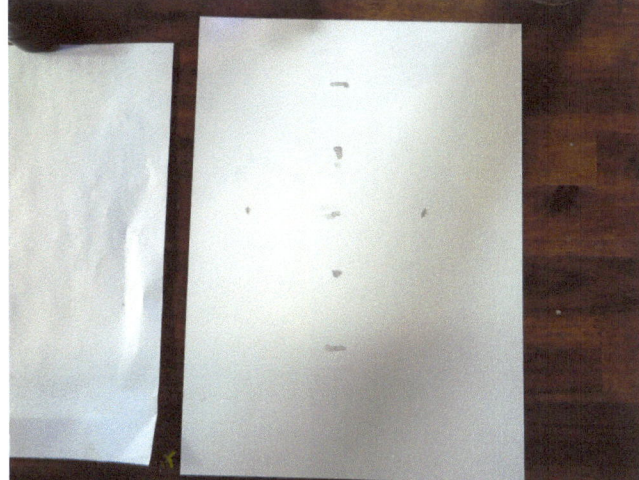

Step 2

Dip your bamboo brush into the ink jar, and then into a cup with water. Test your brush on paper until your ink wash is quite diluted (see the lowest mark on the paper to the left in this photo).).

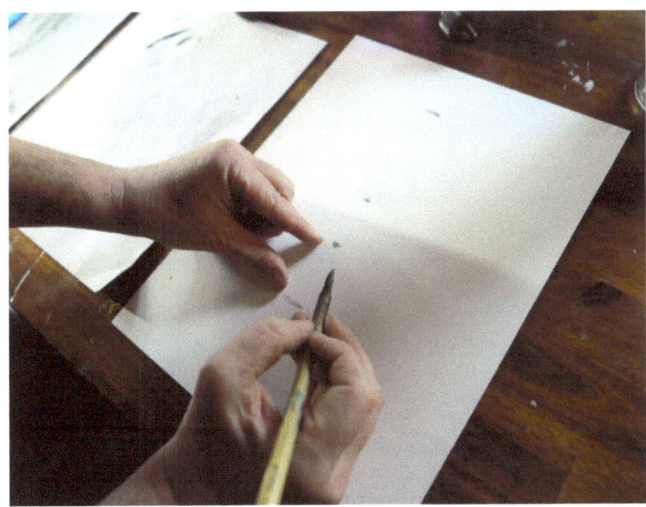

Step 4

Using the measuring method listed on page 24, check the distance of your midline against your vertical line bisecting the face. Remember, once you've determined the length of the midline, then divide it into five equal eye spaces to locate the eyes.

Step 3

Using the diluted wash, mark the top of the head on your paper, then the bottom, and then the three halfway points you found on your source. Use a ruler, or your fingers as demonstrated in the photo!

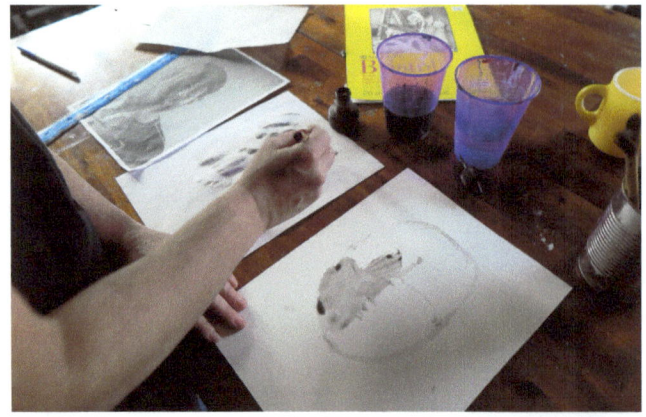
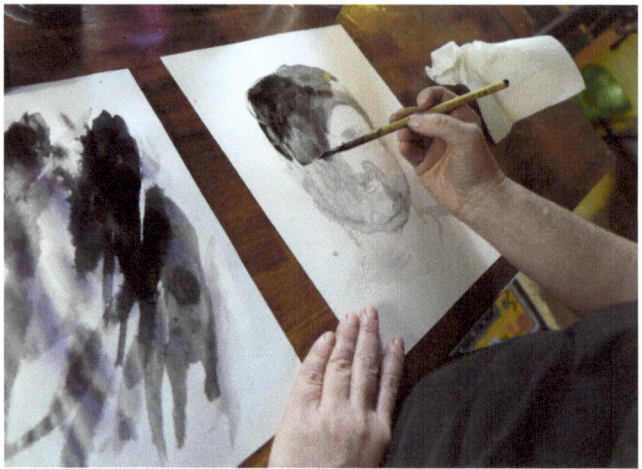
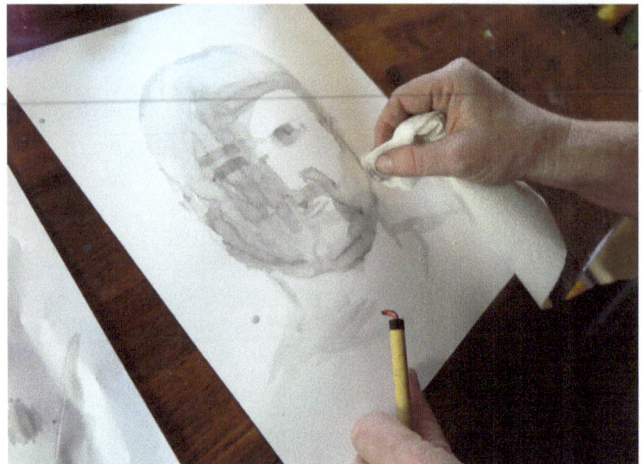
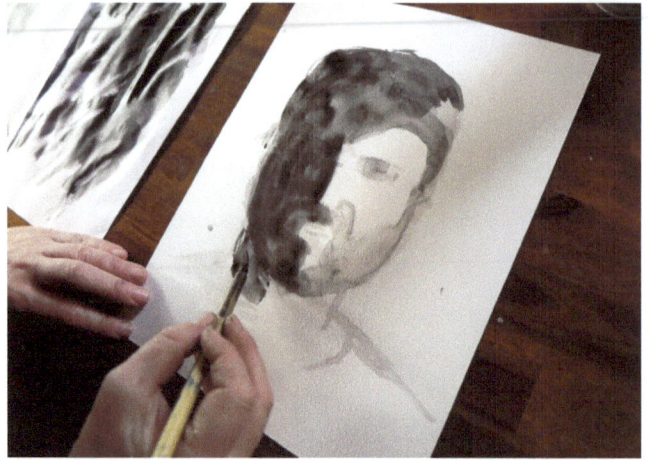
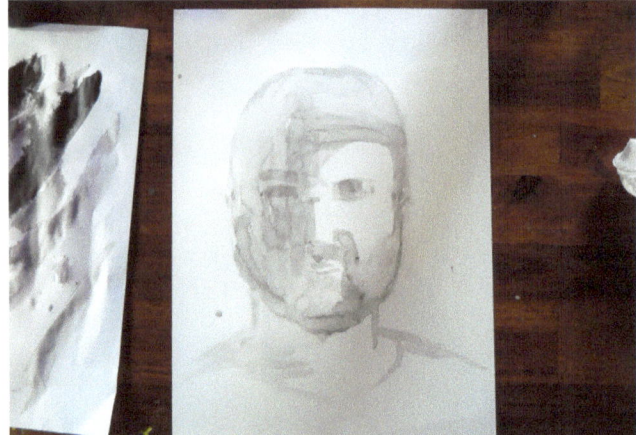
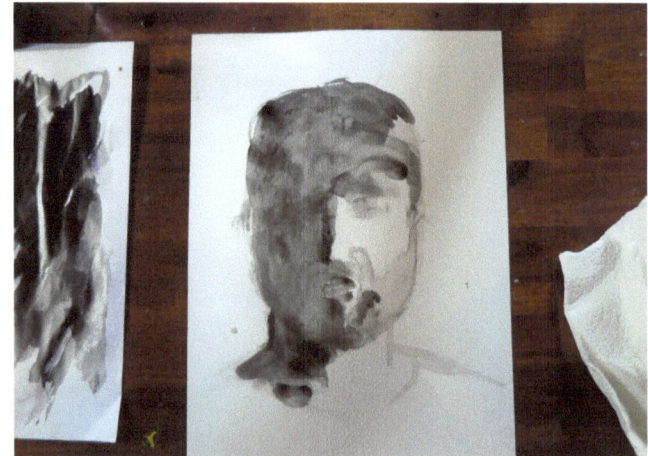

Step 5a-c
still using the very light wash (and constantly testing on the test paper before laying the brush on your bristol paper), paint in the darkest areas of the face. Use a slightly dampened paper towel to dab off excess ink if you stray into a lighter area, as shown in photo 5b.

Step 6 a-c
When you feel more sure of where the features are located, go into the areas with darker ink (you might still dilute it, but not so heavily). Always go to the darkest areas first.

The roaming studio's step-by-step guide to drawing faces

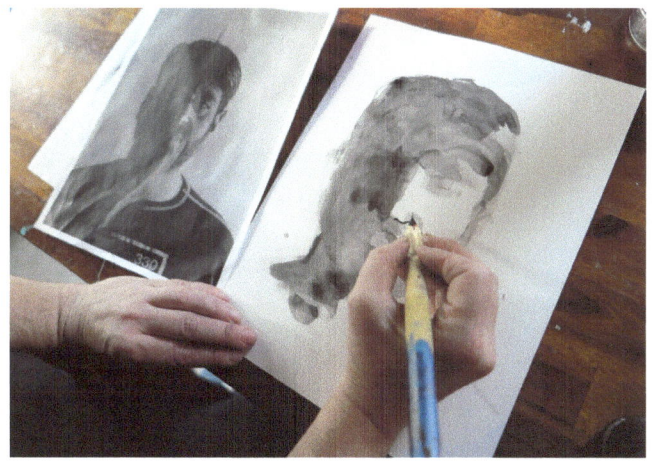
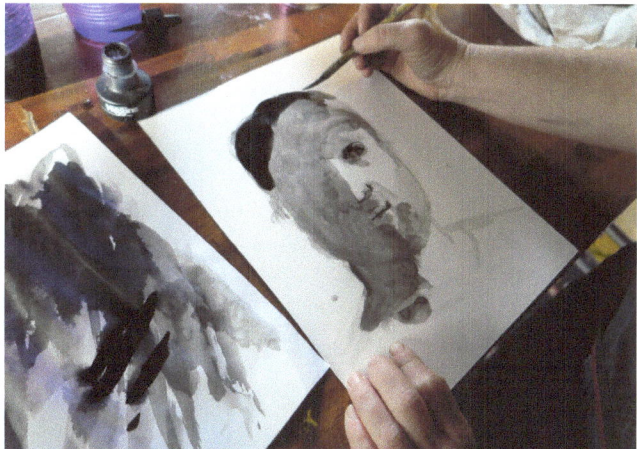
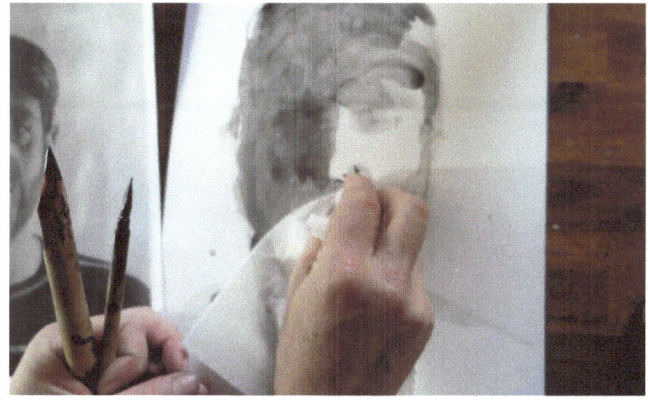
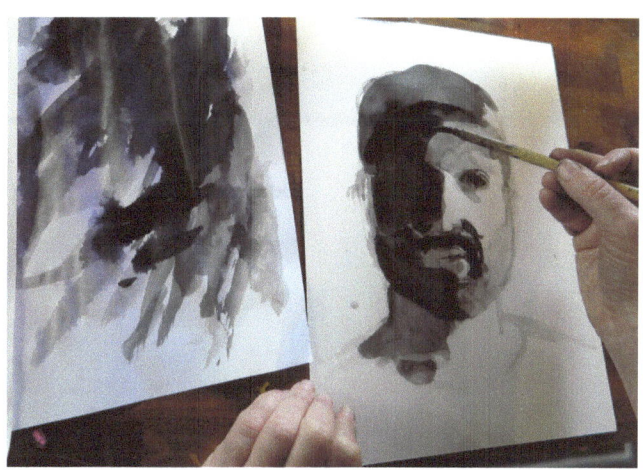
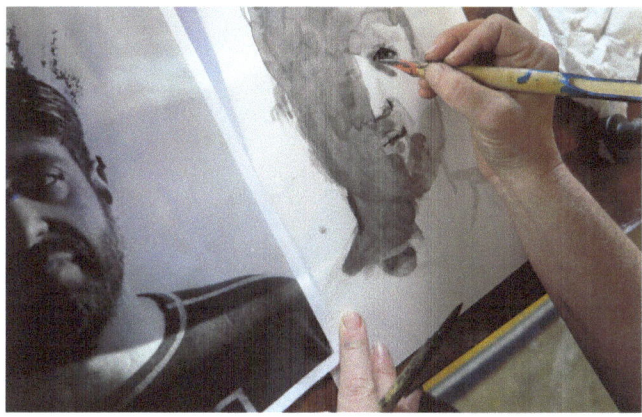
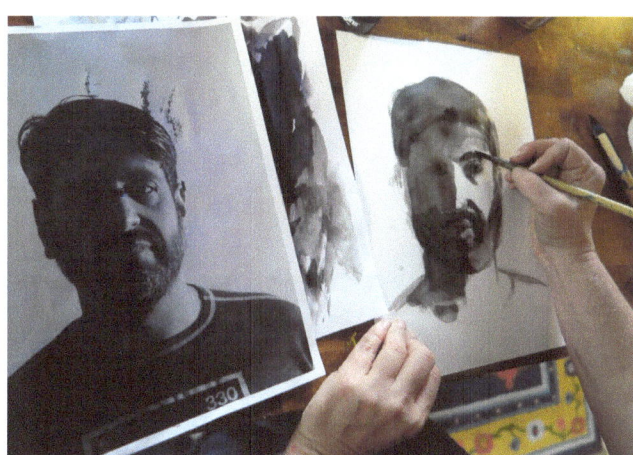

Step 7 a-c

At this point, you can go into a very few areas with the bamboo pen to use strong contour lines. I myself believe in as few strong contour lines in the face as possible, so after I lay down a line (by dipping my pen directly in the ink, testing it and then going directly to the paper), I soften it by lightly scrubbing with a paper towel or a moistened brush. The middle lip line, the eye lines and the outer nostril and base of the nose are the only strongly contoured lines of the face.

Steps 8 a-c

Now is the time to add undiluted ink, with a brush, to the darkest areas of the face.

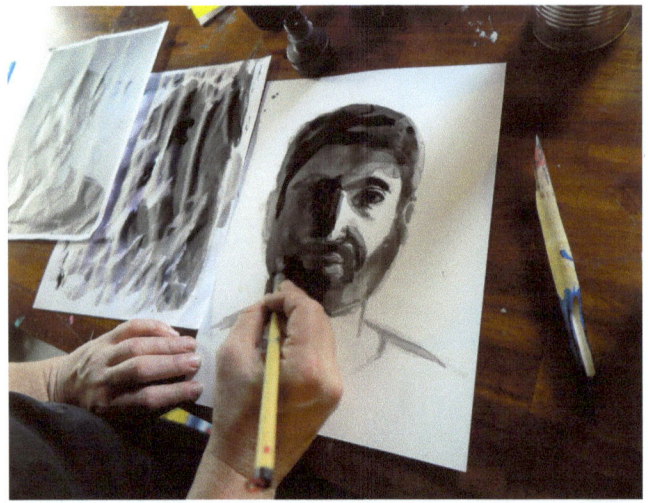

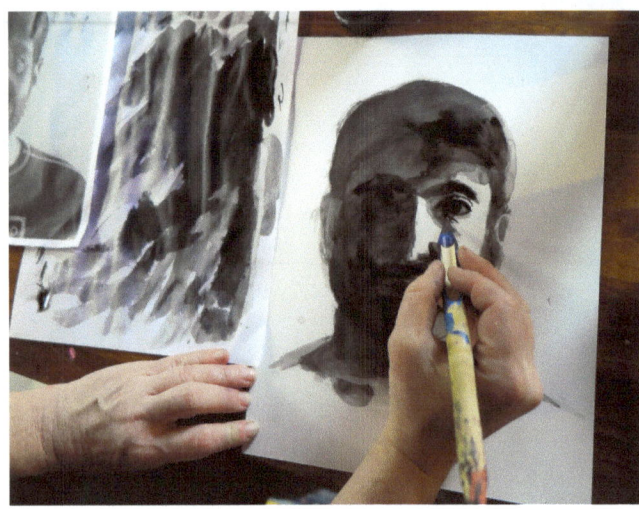

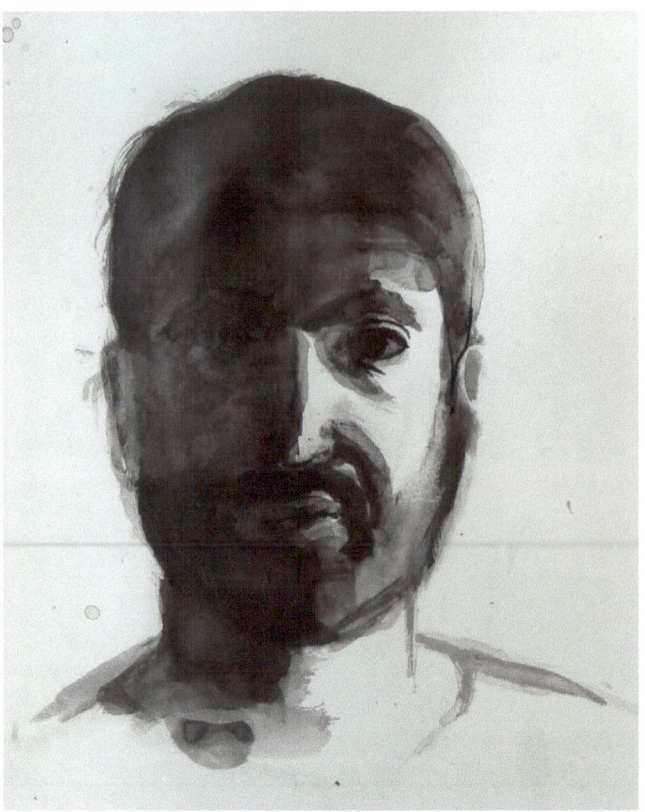

Step 10
Ink is not as correctable as pencil or charcoal, so there is much less back and fourth on these drawings. In the end, you'll note I used the bamboo pen to outline the hairline on the light side. You can use these contour lines for accents as you like, as well.

Steps 9 a-b
I go back over the with the brush and bamboo pen, smoothing out areas and strengthening lines as needed.

This book was published by KikoPro who create beautifully illustrated books for children and adults. KikoPro stories change lives. If you have a book idea email us on info@kikopro.com

If you'd like to have the author of this book critique your drawings, you can book a live online session with her via Skype. One hour of critique and lessons, including reviewing your drawings, costs $75.
Go to theroamingstudio.com for more details
or E-mail: leah@theroamingstudio.com
to register for a lesson.

THE CREATIVE TEAM

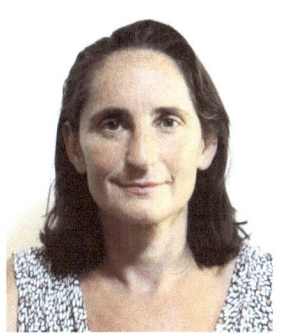
Author
Leah kohlenberg

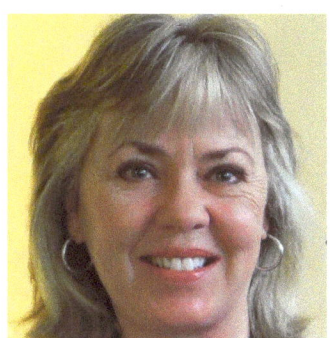
Photography
Stephanie Wiarda

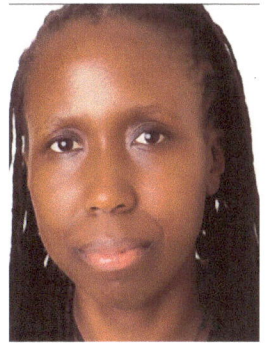
Publisher
J. C. Niala

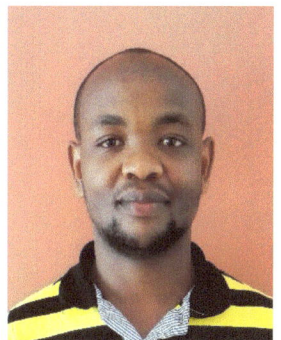
Design & Layout
Kennedy kamau